The
Digital Plan

By

Brad A Schenck

ISBN-13: 9781541144323

ISBN-10: 1541144325

YOUR PATH TO A STRATEGIC DIGITAL PLAN

Table of Contents

Brad A Schenck

Thank You

This book is a manifestation of community on many levels. The material in here didn't just come from magic - it came from years of support and collaborative working and campaigning. Here are just some of the Special Thanks to people who helped make it possible on the way. First to Gus Moore the person who supported me through my first paid "new media" digital work at www.MiamiBeach411.com. Maria De Los Angeles who was an inspiring co-creator when I was first learning online content. Betsy Hoover who gave me the opportunity to merge my content and organizing worlds for President Obama. The entire Obama and Democratic National Committee teams that dreamed, worked, and created change together. Lindsey Allen and Rainforest Action Network team that was willing to take bold leaps and forge a new vision for digital, especially my communications co-conspirator Christopher J. Herrera. A special Thank You to my partner Susan Dusza Guerra Leksander who supported the project and long days of both campaigning and writing. And for all that find this book impactful, special Thank You to Katrina Alexandra Mendoza, the book's contributing editor. Katrina helped take strategic advice and mold it into the impactful and easy to read work before you.

This book is also about community because friends and collaborators chose to help fund the project when it was still in concept. Here is a special Thank You to that community:

Aharon Wasserman
Amy Stuart of cStreet Campaigns
Anthony Nagatani
Audrey J. Edmonds
Brandyn Keating, Founder and Executive Director of Stronger U.S.
Bhavik Lathia - Friend, campaign strategist, technologist.
Bill Schwulst
Billy Rinehart - Respect, Empower, Include
Brian O'Grady
Candice Dayoan
Carey Jeremiason

Carine Terpanjian
Casey Willits
Chris Coger, Founder of Politech
Christina So
Christopher Herrera
Crystal Ruiz
Cyndy Hernandez
Damian Perez
Dan Carson
Debra Cleaver, Founder and CEO of Vote.org
Devin Brady
Devorah Bry of HoneyRoot in honor of those who need a voice.
Emmelia Talarico of Public Citizen
Eric Shih, Founder of Spendrise
Greg Hauenstein
HardPin Media
Hope Hall
Ian Koski
Igor Limansky
Isaac Green
Jackie Nott, Founder of Sparkly Pony
Dr. Jim Pugh
James Soneman
Jason Hoekstra
Jeff Gabriel
Jenn Brown
Jesse Bacon
Jesse Thomas, VP of Product Crowdpac
Jessica Morales Rocketto
Joe McLaughlin
Joe Graeff
Josh Burstein
Joshua Norris, Principal Consultant at Organize Virginia
Justin R. Wilkins of Change Driven Strategies, LLC
Jason Waskey in honor of the OFA Family
Kathryn Reid Moore
Kathryn Schenck
Katrina Alexandra Mendoza in honor of cultivating community interactions.
Kittipon Leepipattanawit
Kathleen Coffen
Laura Callen, Director of The Adoption Museum Project

Lauren Balog Wright
Laura Wilson Fallsgraff
Liz Ruben, Founder of Ecodeo
Marcus T. Coleman Jr
Mario Flores
Marisa Mormile
Matthew Darlison
Matthew Saniie
Maude Baggetto
Melissa H. Gallahan
Michael Lucas
Natalie Foster
Natalie Foster
Rachel Kate Miller
Raje Shwari
Ryan Gallentine
Robyn C. Donaldson, J.D., of Robyn's Healthy Living.
Ross Morales Rocketto
Emmy Ruiz
Sara El-Amine
Sasha Fornari
sooshii
Stacy Cohen
Susan Ito of The Adoption Museum Project
Susan Dusza Guerra Leksander
Tiina Knuutila, Founder of Present Media
Trent Schacht
Vance Hickin
Xavier Moisant

Brad A Schenck

Introduction

For the past five years, I've received emails every few weeks with a request for a digital plan template. My response if often that there aren't great one-stop plans and to date, I've written and coached others to draft hundreds of digital plans. The reason is, it really depends on what the goals are. As you might imagine, the digital plan for the following goals look pretty different:

Is your goal to launch a video or book?

Is your goal to recruit people to an event?

Is your goal to register people to vote?

There are overlapping elements with these goals, but without knowing the specific goals and resources of your project, a template without guidance would likely lead you astray because it would contain unnecessary elements. Every time I receive a request for a template, I tell people I care about that it wouldn't be right for me to send a plan from another project because it won't get you what you need. It is because there are so many issues that I care about and too little of my time to go around that I'm writing this book.

The goal of this book is to empower people like you to make informed decisions and insightful plans that advance your mission. It's designed to give you the proper knowledge to ask the right questions, apply planning best practices, and draft your own plan that achieves the goals you want.

A Story About Planning in the 2012 Democratic Primaries

It's 1:30 AM on a weeknight in January 2012. I've just closed my laptop and I'm trying to fall asleep, but my phone is ringing. It's the Digital Director from Nevada - I groggily ask what's going on and maybe why I'm being called at 1:30 AM. For a few weeks my mind has been bouncing between Eastern, Central, and Western time zones for the states I'm supporting and my Chicago home; South

Carolina, Florida, and Nevada all have a primary or caucus this month.

Primaries and caucuses work different from state to state, which may have become very clear in the 2016 election cycle. In every state it works a little differently, and the dates are set between the political parties and the legislature. In many states, the two parties do not primary or caucus on the same day. So we were really looking at a South Carolina Republican Primary, Nevada Democratic caucus, and Florida Republican primary. In none of these states would Republicans and Democrats share the same day. I am just back from South Carolina, so my internal clock is telling me it's actually 2:30 AM.

Again, why am I being called? It turns out, it has something to do with a flyer that the director can't edit and also can't reach his designer. I'm massaging my temples. South Carolina had been a tough slog of meetings and planning. You might be curious knowing that Democrats don't typically campaign to win South Carolina. It would be fair to ask why we were there focusing on a Republican primary. It simply was part of a larger strategy that involved building energy in South Carolina and translating that into engagement in North Carolina. So I am short to the point in this discussion: "You need to figure this out. It's almost 2 AM here." With push back, I am struggling to grasp what the expectation of this call really is. There is a help center for the Adobe product he is struggling with. I tell him to work on it and I'll talk to him in the morning.

Moral of this story: We were in this position because this director didn't have a plan. The Director hadn't started with the goals around the caucus and worked backward to determine what would be needed to get there. It was a day-to-day frazzled series of actions, and when you operate that way, you find yourself without the systems you need to get things done in a reasonable way.

If you are reading this, you've probably found yourself in one of several positions. You are in direct control of an organization's communications, you are part of a digital team or you are driving a project and you need a plan. You'll also find this handy if you are a leader within an organization or company and want to know where to begin or which questions to ask to make sure your organization is on track. Whether you're on a small campaign, in an organization or simply need to figure this digital business out, in the pages that follow, here is what you will find:

- Guidance and thoughtful questions you should ask.
- Bullet points and lots of them. Planning should at least be succinct.
- Templates that will help you frame your plan.
- Guidance and anecdotes from someone who has helped write and offered advice on hundreds of digital plans.

There is no substitute for intentional planning which is why one-size-fits-all templates don't truly work. This means there are a few things you won't find in this book:

- A silver bullet to success.
- Exact directions on how to use Twitter, Facebook, or any other digital tool, because every organization is different and the tools will change by the time this gets in your hands.
- A plan you can take and just plug your organizational name into.

The chapters that follow walk you through a number of areas that are often rolled into digital departments or digital plans. Depending on the scale of your project or organization, ownership of these elements may live in other departments. For the purpose of this book, we've laid out the chapters to give you the building blocks for a holistic and strategic digital plan. Each chapter can be read on its own or as a building block for a broader plan. We've left margins wide enough for some notes in the print version because we hope you use this book as an ongoing reference for your work.

In some sections you'll see links to the website www.TheDigitalPlan.com for expanded or updated information. We look forward to building out resources and further tips there. Be sure to stop by and sign-up for updates to get the latest in digital strategy for political campaigns, nonprofits, and projects. With the chapter by chapter building blocks and templates, you should be well on your way to creating a strategic digital plan and making positive change in the world.

Goals

At its core, this is a book about Goals.

How to ask the right questions to pick the right goals.

How to make a plan to get to those goals.

With the focus of Goals in mind, you'll see the word "goals" mentioned again and again throughout the book. Time and time again, what I see people struggle with the most in digital work, is defining their goals. Without that definition, people spend a lot of energy (and often money) on work and movement that doesn't get them where they want to go. To make a good digital plan you need to know your specific goals and focus on drafting a plan to meet them.

It's important not to just have big lofty goals, but to be able to break them down into actionable steps and milestones. This section will give you the framework for the milestones and the sections of the book will help you work through the actionable steps. If you feel like you have a solid grasp on the function of goals in planning, go ahead and skip to structure.

Goals — Why you need them

Digital is part science and part art. The part most important to your actual plan is the science. Good digital is built around the science or technical side, great digital is both art and science, and mediocre digital work is often when you focus on only the science or art side. I've met and talked to plenty of people that have a digital, new media, or communications department that don't have clear and specific goals. Making videos, building websites, and sending some tweets are not goals, and they don't serve as a good plan. Digital tools are the means by which you and your organization will accomplish your goals.

During the 2012 cycle, we had three main goals for the digital department: raise money, win votes, and get more volunteers to fulfill the campaign's field mission. If we couldn't clearly tie an action to one of those three things, we did not do it. Goals acted as the starting point from which all of our actions were based. You will have moments with the luxury of creative time and other moments of pure execution within your goals and plan. A good digital plan and team are masters of goals and focus on them well to move progress forward.

Smart goals start with the pinnacle and work their way backwards into a plan. It should never go the other way. Our main campaign goal in 2012 started with getting Barack Obama re-elected. What that truly meant was moving a core group of voters in the battleground states and maintaining the electoral votes in the traditionally blue states. The digital team had the big-picture goals mentioned above - raise money, win votes, and get more volunteers to do the voter outreach. Each of these main goals was broken down into sub-goals and department-specific goals. What actions would work towards these goals as a web-developer, graphic designer, ad buyer, or videographer?

Unless each staffer of your digital team knows what the specific goals of the organization are and how they relate to their role, it is pretty easy to head down rabbit holes where people do cool things but don't meet the greater campaign goals. A plan with clearly defined goals not only keeps your team on track, it also helps with tough conversations around performance evaluations. Finding yourself in the scenario where people are working on projects that aren't mission critical while critical pieces go unattended, can be avoided when everyone knows the mission, its goals, and their part in it.

All too often, many organizers find themselves in one of two places: either the organization's goals are clear but how to break them down into digital roles is not, or the digital and the art of communication roles are defined, but might actually be missing the mark on the mission critical goals. The questions below are to help you avoid the above scenarios, and I recommend you don't do anything until you can clearly answer them.

Goals: What is the goal of this organization or project?

This should be one simple goal like electing Barack Obama, raising awareness about an issue, or producing a film.

What are the subgoals of the organization?

For example: Top-level goal of electing Barack Obama would have these sub-goals:

- Getting to 270 electoral votes by winning in X number of states
- Raising enough money to do that.
- Persuade and turn out enough votes.
- Organize enough volunteers and staff to do that.

Raising awareness about X Issue.

- Have legislation introduced in X state by the end of the year.
- Raise the online conversation by X percentage.
- Have the issue mentioned in the media X number of times by the end of the year.

Now that you know the big overarching goals, you have to decide what the goals of your digital program will be. Section by section, we'll be dissecting the nuanced questions you should be asking for each of the components of your plan. We will start with the big goals that drive decision-making. Ideally, you will have no more than three to five big goals. Your individual teams will certainly have more. Here are some examples of what this could mean:

The 2012 campaign digital team had three main goals:

Raise money, win votes, and get more volunteers to fulfill the campaign's field mission.

— Each department and project had its own goals.

How the video team would approach each of these goals would look pretty different from how the Digital Ads team would approach the same goals. In video, individuals were tasked with creating videos that intertwined persuasion around issues with personal story. The goals there would be around tailoring content to intended segments of voters and getting those voters to view the video. While the Ads team would take many nuanced approaches, they might be looking at placing said video content for persuasion or creating entirely different distilled graphic placement strategy to also win votes.

— Battleground states had their own plans with goals.

Here we are getting down to the brass tacks. Each state would know their likely universe of voters to register. That would, to some degree, change the goals on how many voters they needed to focus on for new voter GOTV (Get Out The Vote), versus likely voters, versus those still in the persuadable category. Along with this, they needed to have specific goals for the kind of earned media they think will help with both GOTV and persuasion. But none of the GOTV is going to happen unless they know how many contacts each volunteer makes per shift and how many staff plus volunteers it will take to reach the voters needed.

— — That states digital team had a section of that plan.

The state team would then need to layer in how emails, tweets, web pages, and online organizing were needed to align support in reaching those goals. Things like recruiting new volunteers, and building for events to meet the capacity goals. As well as things like direct asks to register to vote and trainings for how volunteers could use online tools to register others to vote.

— — — That team had its own set of goals to meet those goals.

This is where the team would breakdown volume and kinds of emails to meet those goals. Calendars of content around deadlines and events.

— — — — Each member of that team should have their own goals.

Individuals would have clear (well campaigns are chaotic, so mostly clear) delineation of what pieces they were responsible for. Who is capturing live content? Who is drafting which email or blog? Who is running which training? Individual goals should be spelled out for the individuals.

If you're thinking that's a lot of goals, you're right! But it's essential to make sure every labor hour is directed at what is needed to win an election or move an issue. Let's say you're creating the digital plan for an issue-driven organization. Your digital goals could look something like this:

Issue organization digital team:

- Tell the story of the Issue.
- Engage and build the supporter base.
- Drive action to move the issue.

Why isn't Tweeting or building a website part of the one of these goals? That's because those things are tactics and tools for meeting goals. You might see goals like post tweets or create X number of videos in a more detailed section of a plan, but it shouldn't be the main vision of a department. Knowing the difference between goals and tools or tactics is critical because completing a tactic might feel like a positive step forward, but if it doesn't change a broader goal you haven't moved the mission.

Benchmarks & Milestones: The Roadmap to Meeting Goals

Identifying the main goal is the first step. One of the biggest failures in planning I've seen, is people working in digital, nonprofit, or campaign operations without clear benchmarks or milestones. I often use the benchmarks and milestones interchangeably. Think of them as guideposts or markers on your way to meeting the big goals.

Lack of benchmarks or milestones leads to confusion, lack of accountability, and often failure. You need these guideposts to know if you are on or off track and why. Teams that use benchmarks and milestones have less confusion over where they are headed. Good benchmarks that are checked in on, allow a team to know if they are achieving the intended productivity and help to optimize the impact in the world they want.

I know it can be tough to develop goals and benchmarks for the first time. That is why this book will walk you through the questions to get you to the right goals, and I'll provide suggestions for benchmarks and milestones you can create and customize to your specific goals.

A Story About Good and Bad Benchmarks and Milestones

During a planning session in spring of 2012, I sat down with a new Digital Director in a battleground state. They were very talented in video production and field organizing, but new to social media and digital plan writing. We had gotten into the piece of his plan where we were talking about Twitter growth. We already knew that if we grew our account and engaged local voters, we could expand the online discussion, recruit more volunteers, and potentially persuade more voters. The plan had a goal of around 3,000 new followers for the quarter. I asked where the number came from and what the benchmarks were.

The number was simply what had happened in prior quarter and they hadn't thought about benchmarks at all. The next draft of the plan included the 3,000 followers very nicely and evenly broken down by month. That may have made me cringe even more. It did not take external factors into account and it did not reflect any ambition for the program. It appeared as if programmatically, there wasn't anything that was going to impact the growth goal. Every organization has something that will make an impact, and numbers rarely run a flat line. Whether it is press, or running an ad, a proactive campaign has certain events or circumstances that impact the numbers. Even the smallest environmental nonprofit sees a surge on Earth Day and can be the local go-to for that day. Others run large ad campaigns that put their brand and online presence into the minds of consumers. Good plans should reflect and account for these impacts.

I told him to make the number aspirational but realistic. What if we made the number 7,000? They said great and made 7,000 the number. I asked him how he'd get there. That's where a qualitative plan and quantitative plan met to create real benchmarks. Would it be a gradual ramp up? Would it have growth points and plateaus? The benchmarks should lay in clear goals and the milestones were the markers of when those goals will be met or significant events and actions impacting the project. That director has since gone on to be a Netroots speaker.

Benchmarks allow you to do two things:

First, they help you evaluate, allocate, and prioritize resources. Second, they allow you to shift goals. If you've met 100% of the quarterly goal after a month, what do you do? Do you merely shift your end quarterly goal higher? Do you reallocate human capital and resources to another project? Or do you double down and add resources because that project is yielding good returns? There may not be a clear right answer and there are many next moves. The only thing you can't do is just ignore the benchmark.

Benchmarks can sound abstract. Here is some guidance on ways to think about benchmarks and as we go through chapters you'll get a stronger perspective on how to set benchmarks for your goals.

> **Percent to goal benchmark -** It's a numerical breakdown of where you need to be at the end of the project. These work well when everyone who needs to read the plan knows the end goals. These are also helpful when you need to move in small increments. For example, while working with a really diverse range of Facebook pages, at one point my team collectively decided that 3-5% growth over the quarter is what we wanted. But for some accounts, that meant only acquiring a few hundred fans, while for others, it meant thousands. Using the % made it easier for everyone to be on the same page on what sustainable growth looked like.

Raw number benchmark - This type of benchmark is similar to percent to goal, but shows the raw number instead of percent. Some numbers are just visually better and can feel more impactful when going over the raw numbers. While plotting out a map for what we expected for online voter registration in Nevada, we had an end goal of 10,000. But this wasn't going to be linear growth. The numbers were going to jump wildly depending on ad buys, election cycle timing, and major events we were creating. Understanding that our benchmarks would move in very steep spikes and jumps, as opposed to an inaccurate linear graph, clarified our path to achieving our goal.

The milestone - Some goals aren't numerical and that's when you need the milestone. This could be finalizing a contract with a vendor. Things like securing materials needed for a project. This could be a sub piece of the project being finished, like the script for a video, a particular piece of a website, or a proposal for that. It's hard to have a percent to goal benchmark on hiring someone or having a contract. Use a milestone instead.

Another Look at the Impossible Goals

While, working with the Democratic National Committee, I had the pleasure of working on a team led by Natalie Foster and Josh Peck. They had the entire New Media team build one large project plan with goals and benchmarks. Most of the team knew their goals and the benchmarks. We would gather once a month to talk about our teams' goals, percent to goal, and the reasons behind the current status. With aspirational planning, if we make it to 100% to goal on 80-90% of our projects, we had really achieved something. Why not 100% you ask? We were relying on aspirational goals raising the bar for everything we were doing. They had a solid grasp of what we needed to achieve to move the mission forward, and getting to the 80-90% marks would mean we hit baseline success. But the plan was about stretching goals and that meant planning for the aspirational 100%. With plans in motion to hit this new 100%, we would stretch ourselves and have a better understanding for what is possible.

Though this type of planning worked for us, I don't think this style of planning works everywhere. You would need top level buy-in on the reasons for charting an aspirational course that may be out of reach. That level of agreement would require consideration around which goals fall into the achievable category and which fall under aspirational. If you need to build trust in your department, I would NOT recommend this kind of planning but actually the opposite. I would shoot for a plan where you exceed 80% of your goals and meet 100%.

Goals: Know Thy Goals and Know Thy Plan

I've watched plenty of people write plans and never internalize the plan or use it as their actual guideposts. Don't get trapped in the idea you are writing the plan for someone else. Sure! It may be needed for your supervisor or a board, but at the end of the day, it's for you or your program.

What I've seen from the most successful organizations is tiers of plans clearly outlined with the top-level goals for the entire organization. Top-level plans shouldn't be digging into all of the rich details needed to execute the tiers below departments, teams, and individuals. Think of that as a plan that is a wide-lens vision of the work for three, six, or 12 months. Something that could easily be read by a board or group of funders. Deeper dives for departments and teams can include more nuanced goals. Then flesh out plans for individuals with goals that clearly build the work of the department or team plan. Those individual team members' plans should be really in the weeds and have many micro benchmarks for them and their projects.

Know what goes behind the benchmarks and final goals. People will ask, or at least they should. If you are the person who should be asking then do. If the plan writer does not have concrete ideas, goals, and benchmarks behind the plan then you're in trouble. This is a major goal of the book, equipping everyone at each stage of plan making to ask the right questions to have clear answers and build a winning plan from there!

Why Tactics Aren't Goals

Goals and tactics are two very different things.

> *Goals are the outcomes that you want to achieve.*
> *Tactics are the actions to get to those goals.*

Consistently, I see people confuse digital tactics with goals. Here is an example of a tactic misplaced as a goal that I often see around the use of video:

> *Our goal is to make a video.*

Your goal could be to raise awareness or get people to join a thing or to donate. But video is the tactical end to either of those goals. The question is, if one of those is the goal, does a video reach that goal for you? Is it part of a broader strategy to reach that goal?

We'll break this down in each section but more often than not, the broad goal should not be a tactical thing, but an impact that is (ideally) measurable.

Structure

The art of writing any good plan is knowing your audience. Often in digital, we use the term audience for the receivers of content and your plan is no different. You will need to make some decisions on who the reader is and how far in the weeds they need information. This will change what the presentational structure will look like because you need a plan that strikes the right balance of information and functionality.

Hopefully you know who your audience is, at least in broad terms. Your audience could be your board, an executive or department director, funder, or staff. You should know what the expectations are of the audience you are delivering to. Are they expecting top lines and bullets, long insightful paragraphs, or some combination of the two? It's your job as the plan writer to be sure you know this information. If you just write a plan and send it off without knowing the expectations of your audience, there is a solid chance you should expect a serious redraft.

Here are a few key questions you should ask about a draft you need to deliver to someone else.

- Is there a maximum or minimum length expected?
- Is there a preferred template the final plan should fit?
- Is the expectation for it to be about top lines and finished products?
- How can you show benchmarks and milestones?
- How can you illustrate the plan without showing all the details?
- How in the weeds do you need to, go (i.e. digital wonk or no wonk)?

Structure: Drafting

Once you have some answers, you should start drafting. The real key is just starting and not worrying too much about the end structure. You will probably find one or both of these to be true:

The final delivery of the plan to an audience not directly executing the work is not likely to be detailed enough to efficiently run a project or program day-to-day.

The structure of the plan might not fit how your brain works.

Start by writing the plan you need to run your program or project. Never constrain what you need to meet goals to a product that needs to be delivered to stakeholders who are not executors. If you only need to deliver a two-page plan but you know your program needs a 20 page in-depth guide with micro benchmarks to the day, then write that plan. Take that 20 page plan, distill it for delivery and use it personally for you and your team to achieve everything you said you'd do. That distilled plan will guide you to success.

Possible Problems with Drafting

An artist, a data scientist, and a web developer walk into a bar... One draws or writes about it. One analyzes it. One considers the user experience of it.

The modern digital team in many organizations is a beautiful mixture of people with very, very different disciplines. Quite literally, your brains work differently.

Artist Meets Drafting

You might be part of a digital team or project because you are a little more creative than many members of your staff. But your brain doesn't see the world the same way your friend in operations does. Maybe you find yourself staring at the template you've been given and it just doesn't work for what you need to do. My advice is don't write it that way. I've run into this exact same problem myself. I've looked at the template and tried to start writing in someone else's structure and it just doesn't work.

Two days later, I walked into a room with a white board and started mapping one piece of my internal plan on a white board. I knew one of the end goals I needed to get to, and I had a calendar of events that led to that goal. But my mind needed the big visual to see the steps and fill in the gaps. Once I felt good with what was on the board, I put it to paper (a word document). I subsequently worked through other pieces and drafted the plan in the structure I am most comfortable with (which is bullets, top lines, and a lot of benchmarks connected to events and days). **I first mapped the plan I needed and then distilled it into what was needed from me.** There was one extra addendum that didn't fit the exact template I was given, but I explained how it was helpful and was thanked for being thoughtful about the process.

The Analytic Meets Drafting

On the flip side you might be a numbers driven person. Everything about benchmarking and milestones that are numerical might be ideal for you, and it's the question of how to quantify the time for the creative side that is the mental block. We'll dig into that a bit more in the sections related to creative processes like writing, design, and video because it takes grounding in the art to make that possible.

Structure: Delivery

If you just need to deliver a straightforward two-page document, then this might be easy enough. Chances are though, you'll need to read through the plan with leadership peers, your supervisor, and at the very least, with the team you're working with. This is the part that goes back to internalizing your plan. If you are working on a large plan where you have other teams writing their piece, you'll want to spend some time with them knowing more deeply what goes into their plan.

If you need to formally present your plan in front a large group, say with a presentation, here are a few tips to make sure you get the buy-in you need and deserve.

Tip #1 on Delivery: Be sleek, data driven, and efficient.

I think of modern digital as these three things. Sleek design builds branding and can drive action. If design lives within your department, then your presentation should be the best looking one on the screen that day.

Data is why digital is real. We have evolved passed the early days of social media and motives such as, "It's about being social, "and "We do it because it gives our brand personality." Nowadays, we either have, or are building, data to make better decisions on quality of impact. You have data on the impact of tools, channels, and investments your team is making and can produce. Share that data, be real with that data. (Also, if you read this book and then present a plan and use the term viral, I will haunt you. I promise my digital ghost will haunt you).

Efficiency: The presentation should be as efficient as possible because part of what the world is looking for from digital tools and technology is efficiency. The final reason people are making these investments in digital is the efficiency it adds to all kinds of engagement and messaging. Digital accomplishes things like building new conversation channels with supporters and consumers because it takes traditional paid advertising like commercials and gives it more depth online, with tracking ability, and a wider reach across social media.

Tip #2 on Delivery: Different isn't always better.

The best example of this that I've witnessed was the Prezi explosion of 2012. A number of people wanted to present something using Prezi but didn't take the time to really understand Prezi. I don't mean the *how* to zoom and pan but *why* to zoom and pan. They looked like a Powerpoint had vomited on a Prezi and zoomed around that mess. I love both traditional slide programs like Powerpoint and Prezi, but they are different and should each be treated with an artistic eye. Most importantly, just adding new flashy things to your presentation doesn't make it better. Same goes for just making the presentation over-stylized, having too many animations (I've been guilty of that), or using additions that may or may not perform 100% every time.

Tip #3 on Delivery: Be Visual.

If you are talking about three million viewers, then you should show a proper representation of three million viewers. Less text is always, always better. If you're talking about Twitter, it could look like a Twitter timeline or Facebook page, Tumblr, Snapchat, Pinterest, or other familiar site. If you are influencing 10,000 voters, show a voter being influenced and the tools that will do it, and use your voice to talk about that. Don't write that all on the board. To put these tips into practice, here are is a checklist to bring it home.

The plan presentation checklist:

- Have I walked through it several times?
- Did a second or third eye copyedit my work?
- Does it work offline if needed?
- Do I know the material?
- Will it play on the device I am using?
- Do I need handouts?

To access templates and more tips for planning structure please visit:

www.TheDigitalPlan.com/plan_templates_and_examples for the current and updated lists.

Staff

So you've got the skeleton of a plan and realize you don't have the staff needed to create it, or you are drafting a plan for a project or department that doesn't even exist yet. It's on you to figure out who you need. As you contemplate this task feeling slightly overwhelmed with stress, you should know you're not alone. Outside of a relatively small but growing group of people, very few people have run a large digital program or enough holistic digital programs to know exactly what they need. Every developer, designer, and social media expert is different. Part of plan writing is getting a sense of who you really need.

Clarifying who you need comes in the form of quality expectation and knowing exactly what it is you are trying to do. I've watched a video team of one-and-half full-time people create 12 videos in eight weeks, and a team of six create four videos in the same number of weeks, but they were producing different videos with different goals. The same could easily be said for social media: I've watched one good person really develop one really engaging twitter account and one good person develop four less engaging accounts. Both cases were strategically correct uses of time, given different goals.

Here are some of the initial questions that should be asked:

- What are the biggest programmatic goals we need to achieve?
- What kind of budget do we have?
- Do we need people that can perform multiple tasks such as video planning (producing), shooting, and editing or people who are focused on just one task like graphic design or shooting?
- Do we need several good generalists (basic html coding, writing, some video editing)?
- At what point do we need managers of people?

Insiders vs. Specialized Skills

This might be a real issue you'll run up against especially if you're in a nonprofit that likes to hire from inside the same organization or field. But if you are running a team inside any institution, you should consider it. Will you hire someone who is loyal to the organization and wants to grow as part of the team, or will you bring in someone from outside? This might sound abstract but should be well considered. I've watched both go well and poorly. Especially if you are an organization with a really specific culture and mission. Here is an example to consider.

> We were hiring state digital directors for the 2012 campaign. We had solid leads of people from inside and outside the organization. There were two candidates in two different states. Both had worked in the field working directly with volunteers so they understood the core mission of the organization at the state level.
>
> Candidate one had a great background with us and had also been managing the state's social networks for that given state. Yet, they didn't have much digital knowledge beyond that. They had a clear aptitude and vision to learn more. In the end, they built one of the best digital programs in one of the most critical battlegrounds. They had the aptitude to plan, write, grow, ask the questions they didn't know, and bring on the people needed to fill gaps.
>
> Candidate two had the field background but also worked in video production. Video is a difficult skill. They knew they lacked the other components like social media strategy, but were eager to learn. They unfortunately had to change roles after two months. It just wasn't the right fit and left us with a gaping hole.

To be honest there is not a magic solution to change candidate two into candidate one. Candidate two was later replaced by someone from outside the organization because the decision was made we didn't have the time to develop someone from the inside.

They quickly understood the culture and applied their knowledge to that culture and program.

One of the biggest factors in choosing whether or not to work from the inside vs. outside is time. Do you have the time to develop someone? Do you believe they'll stay on longer if you do? If you have a small project or limited window, I would - more often than not - hire skills from outside rather than try to develop it from the inside.

An Important Note on Culture

When building a team, you need to decide what is most important for your team culture. I've met some really skilled people who just didn't gel with their team. This actually killed the overall production of a team. It's up to you to set the tone and hire the people that fit that team or, in time, cut the folks that don't fit.

If you are going to build a team of people who just show up and execute and clock out when their project is done, that's fine, but make sure everyone you hire fits that team. The same is to be said if you are trying to build a close-knit team. Don't hire that person who wants to sit in a dark room and edit, code, or write and never talk if collaboration is important to their role and team. If you feel the need to hire someone who might not be a perfect cultural fit, talk to them about it. Make sure you are deliberate and give them the reasons why it might be difficult. I promise you, both you and the hire will be happier either way. The bad scenario is hiring someone with the skills who underperforms because they dislike showing up to their environment. But a great scenario is one where everyone flourishes because you have built an intentional community in your department or project team.

Website and Web Development

The biggest beast of burden for digital teams and projects right now may very well be web development. Here are the three biggest hurdles I've seen and experienced over the years:

1. **Unrealistic scope of project** in funding, timing, need, or ability.
2. **Designing web pages or tools for a small audience** that did not serve the core audience needed to meet larger goals.
3. **Bloat** including bells and whistles distracting from the core website actions you need people to take. Or basically just too many damn things on a page.

Each of these problems and hurdles occur when the goals can't be well defined or put into a hierarchy.

We'll break this part of the book down into a few sections, which will help you figure out a plan. If you are starting a big new project, this might be the hardest goliath you'll encounter of any of the digital planning elements.

It is important to start with asking yourself the question of whether or not to start into a new web development project and if that is the best way to meet your goals. Relative to that will be identifying the type of project you are tackling.

> **A new organization or campaign**
> **A new project**
> **Rebuilding an existing site**

From there you can dig into the processes of planning out your capacity and dig into the structural planning and timelines to make sure the sum of the work and effort adds up to meeting your goals.

Website and Web Development: To build or not to build? That should be the question.

If you are launching a new project or organization not connected to another entity, this question may be fairly straightforward.

But before you start into any project, you need to know: what is your #1 goal? Can you break it down into the top three sub-goals working toward the long-term goals of the organization?

If you are starting from scratch and goal #1 is to build a website, then that seems pretty straightforward.

So let's pause here and split the question into three sections.

Start below for a new organization or campaign, if you are at square one with your project or campaign. Skip down to the section of Web Development called "New Project," if you have an existing website and you are working on a plan for a micro-site, or approaching development for a specific future project. Lastly, if you have a website but need to revamp the entire thing, jump to the "Rebuilding an Existing Site" section.

Website and Web Development: For new organization or campaign

You just need a website. Sounds simple enough but you should answer the next few question before you endeavor to build your website.

> *What needs to happen on the website on day one?*

> *What needs to happen on the website at the 30 day, three month, six month marks?*

> *Do you have capacity to build this in-house or do you need to contract out?*

The question on day one, day 30, three months, six months, and one year will dictate a lot of the planning and work that will need to go into the site. — *(See site planning worksheet at www.TheDigitalPlan.com/SitePlannningWorksheet)*

These factors should impact which web platform you choose since there are a plethora of them out there. *(Instead of publishing a soon-to-be outdated list here, please check out an updated list at www.TheDigitalPlan.com/choosingplatforms).*

The platform options will dictate which CMS (Content Management System) you use. A CMS system is how you post and create website content like a basic page, blog post, or donate page. CMS examples include WordPress, Squarespace, Drupal, Wix, Tumblr, NationBuilder, and more. CRM (Customer Relationship Management) systems can be pretty basic, but for organizational and campaign work it can get more complicated. Some people think of their email client as their CRM. Examples include MailChimp, Constant Contact, and BlackBaud. When choosing the CRM that is right for you, you may want it integrated with some of your site specialty pages like petitions, donate pages, and sign-ups. In this case, you would need something like Blue State Digital, ActionKit, Action Network, Salsa, Convio from BlackBaud, NationBuilder, or EveryAction. But if you are doing deep volunteer management or connecting to a voter file, you will probably have to choose between EveryAction from NGPVAN or NationBuilder. Your head might be spinning now. This is also a major question on how many database tools you'll need to connect. Please take some time and reference the Data and Analytics section.

You might be thinking, *"Whoa we don't have time to decide what we want, we just need a page up next week!"* That's okay too, as long as you know your day one, day 30, three months, six months, and 12 month goals. These milestones are important for you to prioritize how you'll manage the content and building of new pages and tools.

Here are a few examples that may be helpful for you to think through what you'll need at each stage, and how to start the most basic selection process.

The long run is simple —

Let's say you are doing a pretty simple informational campaign and that you'll just want to make basic info available and you aren't driving donations or petitions.

> Day 1: Basic three-page site is live - About Org, About Campaign, Sign-Up
> Day 30: Expanded materials like PDFs and other info
> 3 Month: Basic Updates
> 6 Month: Basic Updates
> 12 Month: Basic Updates

"Basic updates" this might look bland but it is placeholder for information like new blogs, updating your basic information, or pages that exists. It is a recognition that you might not be expecting more development work but just content maintenance. Even if it is a robust series of blogs that should appear in a content calendar not a website production plan.

If this looks like what you need then keep it simple and go with something like WordPress or Squarespace. Stylize a good template and focus on the other work.

Let's say your goals are a little more complicated, and you need donate and event pages. Question here is, do you need them on day one, day 30, or three months in?

It's important to make clear decisions on what you need for day one of the website launch because two different projects could look like the following:

> Scenario #1
> Day 1: Basic three-page site is live - About Org, About Campaign, Sign-Up
> Day 30: Donate page live, Blog Live, Events pages live
> 3 Month: News Releases Live
> 6 Month: Updates to homepage, About page
> 12 Month: Basic updates continue

> Scenario #2
> Day 1: More robust site is live About Org, About Campaign, Sign-Up, Donate page live, Blog live, Events pages live, News Releases Live,

Day 30: Updates to homepage; Capacity to update all functions continue
3 Month: Basic updates continue
6 Month: Basic updates continue
12 Month: Basic updates continue

These two scenarios might look pretty similar but the outcomes can be drastically different. Consistently in the past, people new to web development often want Scenario #2 because they believe it is best to have everything all at once. That means done and ready. But websites are rarely done. Everyone who knows anything about website development will tell you it's about ongoing updates and iterations.

To make Scenario #2 a reality, the project planner might say, *"We'll just add capacity or start earlier."* But this doesn't really account for focus and testing. You aren't just gaining time in what has to be produced in Scenario #1. You are gaining quality and affording yourself the testing of your product with better review of content for all responsible parties. That quality and testing will also apply to what gets delivered at the day 30 mark. By allowing the production team to just focus on a few key elements, you should get better looking, well-tested, and edited content. Then focus on updating that content in the first week or two after being live. You'll learn some things to apply to the next round of pages.

Now let's create a more in-depth scenario.

Scenario #3
Day 1: Basic three-page site is live - About Org, About Campaign, Sign-Up
Day 30: Donate page live, Blog live, News Releases live
3 Month: Petitions pages live, Events pages live
6 Month: Integration with CRM for volunteer management
12 Month: Basic updates continue

I would recommend looking closely at the goals at each of these time milestones and ask what is flexible. What can't be lost and what is connected to an external deadline. Every feature you add that involves a database, should be considered very carefully and only chosen according to whether you can do it with one unified database of tools, or if you'll need many.

Real Life Processes -- Priorities and Long-Term Solutions

On a major project I am consulting on, we scoped out for an organization that wanted to be doing community organizing. We were able to separate the short-term needs from the long-term needs, and create a web development plan from there. The plan looked a little like this:

> Day 1: Basic three-page site is live - About Org, About Campaign, Sign-Up
> Day 30: Hiring page and other simple info pages up
> 3 Month: Donate page live, Events pages live, Blog live, News Releases live, Integration with CRM for volunteer management
> 6 Month: Petitions pages live
> 12 Month: Build out more in-depth issue pages

In this scenario, the events and data integration were major priorities because the top goals of the organization were to do in-depth community organizing around issues. You might ask, *"If those were the top goals, then why didn't it happen in the first 90 days?"* It's about being realistic about whether or not something is a real priority. If it needs to work well over time and grow, you should work toward the best long-term solution.

One of the key audiences we needed to build for the first 90 days was comprised of major donors and funders. The initial push for volunteers would happen in three to four months after the first pages needed to be up. In this particular case, we didn't even build the site on the same system, because long term, we would need a well-integrated database that allowed for emailing, volunteer management, voter file data, and petitions. We decided we would give ourselves the time to set that all up properly. We would start with a light lift, easy out-of-the-box site template, and get basic info out into the world. From there, we would build out the in-depth site we needed later.

This is why knowing the goals for several major milestones is so key. It allows you to avoid rushing work that needs quality time and it ensures you make the right decision on resources both short term and long term.

Website and Web Development: New project

By now, you have some framing on how to think about some key milestones for day one, day 30, three month, six month, and 12 month goals. Next, you are going to need to figure out the resources to get there.

The new project. It has you excited because you are kicking off a new campaign! It's going to be the best yet, with bigger goals, a bigger impact and that means you are going to do things like you've never done them before. You are going to build something awesome and new because…

Here is your key question. *What is the goal of the web development?*

I've been a part of hundreds of sub campaign pushes from voter registration drives and email campaigns to corporate targets, photo-petitions, micro-sites for one key message, and launching big campaigns that need a full new site.

In all of these cases, you really need to begin by asking: *What is the campaign goal?*

From that answer, sub-questions develop:

> *What do we need to impact to meet that goal?*

> *How have we or others done this before?*

Once you answer that, you need to know: *For Web Development, our top goal is… and our three sub-goals are [1], [2], [3].*

Someone who understands web development should be consulted as early as these campaigns goals are decided. Too many times, I've watched people without web development experience go into planning and get really excited about their ideas. And too many times, I've watched people get wedded to ideas without consultation and (more often than not) the product doesn't meet their goal. The times when web developers have been in the room early on, I've seen it consistently lead to a far better product that meets goals and moves the needle on change.

To make these kinds of decisions, you should be able to make a distinction between the following things:

Website: Any multi-page site on the internet regardless of the functions on the site.

Micro-site: A page with less than five pages, and often as little as one to three pages. And if it has more than three functions, it is probably a small website and not a microsite. If it's hosting images, a donation page, and a sign-up page, that's a website.

Web tool or application: Folks often get confused here and mostly think of phone apps. But this would typically be anything that renders or captures data or allows someone to take an action. Basic web pages typically show static information and images or videos that stay constant unless updated on the backend. If the user can make a selection that renders different data on screen, or submit info that sends to a target, or they have a data-driven profile, web tools or applications are in use. The distinction is they are typically harder to create and manage long-term.

Sub-section of a site: This could have a distinct look and feel to the main site. It could even have a different URL that directs you there, but it's built on the same backend and layout of the site.

These distinctions are critical to good planning because they clarify the specific resources needed to build and maintain your website.

New Project: Capacity

It's important to be realistic and carefully consider the tradeoffs. There are always some.

A big question you need to ask: "Is there in-house capacity or do we need to look for outside support?"

If you believe there is in-house capacity, you should know what the trade offs are. Will it mean holding off on other updates or will basic edits get deprioritized? Make sure everyone is aligned on the tradeoffs.

Here are a few tips:

> Make sure you know how basic troubleshooting is going to happen during the special project phase.

> If you are bringing in outside support limit their point of contact to one or two people. Group calls can be fine but even with just two people you will have some conflicting input.

> An important part of web development timelines is making sure there is time for delays. I've watched many missed deadlines occur because the preliminary deadlines were overly optimistic. Make sure everyone involved has accounted for at least a day of delay at each milestone.

Website and Web Development: Rebuilding an existing site

Now this is a doozy. I was around for the rebuild of several iterations of BarackObama.com and led RAN.org through two rebuilds in two years. The planning here is very similar to planning for a new organization but with different considerations. A major tip I shared with someone starting a rebuild at another organization: **You need to manage day-to-day operations or manage the website project - don't do both.** Both require a high amount of capacity. Either bring in contract support to keep day-to-day operations going, or bring in contract support to make the site happen. Doing both will most likely mean you won't be able to do either very well.

When rebuilding an existing site, your main question around goals is more nuanced, but very similar to what you need on day one.

I've seen minimal iterative design work go well and I've seen it go poorly. When the team relaunched Obama 2012, it was very stripped down and minimal. It did not link to the years of blogs and content the supporters had built up. While that ruffled many feathers, the main goal of giving the campaign a fresh look and feel was achieved by cutting off past content. It gave the press a reason to cover a campaign launch they knew was inevitable because it was a sleek new look and feel for the campaign, and not a sprawling five years of organizing website.

I recommend having very clear day one, day 30, three month, six month, and one year milestone markers. In a recent relaunch I worked on, we didn't have all of this laid out well and it meant that the struggle to bring back online organizational resources we needed became an intra-organizational struggle. Learn from this example and please don't repeat this mistake. Consult with other organizations that have gone through this. Not sharing expectations of when features will return will create internal turmoil instead of relief of having a modern site. Lay it out on the timeline and take everyone along on the path.

Website and Web Development: Capacity and Planning

We've laid out a few buckets with which to frame the kinds of website development projects you might encounter. However, the only way to make any of them happen is to be honest about capacity and planning. Capacity and planning are a bit of a chicken and an egg scenario. They both have the ability to dictate what is possible, and one doesn't necessarily come before the other.

Capacity is about internal staff and budget. If these are initial constraints, then start here. If your project is more about scoping, determining budget and answering capacity needed, then start at planning. Here are a few views of realistic capacity as of Fall of 2016:

> **Building a fully functioning website that is content rich.**
> Working with quality development firms will cost $30,000 and up, and take about three months or more to be done well.

A team of one web developer, designer, content writer, and project manager working full-time on launching a full site might need most of their capacity for three months. That same team with other ongoing projects should have at least six months to work on the project in parallel.

Building a basic site with just a few pages and functions.

Working with quality development firms will cost around $10,000 and up, and take about a month or more to be done well.

A team of one web developer, designer, content writer, and project manager working full-time on launching a full site might need most of their capacity for a month or two depending on internal review processes. That same team with other ongoing projects should have at least two to three months to work on the project in parallel.

Building a true microsite, or main site special project, or a very basic first pages of a website.

Working with quality development firms will cost around $3,000 - $5,000 depending on visual design and content and will take about a month or more to be done well.

A team of one web developer, designer, content writer, and project manager working full-time on launching a full site might need most of their capacity for two to four weeks depending on internal review processes. That same team with other ongoing projects should have at least three to five months to work on the project in parallel.

Hopefully the microsite piece helps you understand and plan for concurrent projects if you are at a large or midsize organization running multiple campaigns or projects. Don't plan on more than one special project at a time unless you are bringing in capacity for more development, design and other skill sets, either in-house or via contractors.

Project Planning for Web Development

My recommendation for a process to plan:

> Step 1: Know your Goals
> Step 2: Scope your project
> Step 3: Develop project plan
> Step 4: Execute project plan
> Step 5: Review goals in relation to executed project. Learn.

Step 1: Know Your Goals

This is covered above and you can use www.TheDigitalPlan.com/SitePlannningWorksheet but make sure you've got the following down:

> You understand your needs and your #1 Goal. You also know the top three subgoals and the long-term goals of the organization.
>
> You know what needs to happen on the website on day one.
>
> You know what needs to happen on the website at the 30 day, three month, six month and even one year marks.

Use the worksheet and ongoing tips at: www.TheDigitalPlan.com/SitePlannningWorksheet

Step 2: Scope Your Project

This is the time to dig into what you really want. It's discussing what is behind the goals of the development and what you want the site to look and feel like. Look and feel aren't some hippy dippy concept there are the cornerstone of User Experience (UX). Take this very seriously, it can make or break a project.

Take time to look at other sites and understand what you like and dislike about their design and function. Make a living document of it. Come together and discuss it.

Then make sure you are working with a qualified web developer and designer who can look at different designs and use that to influence your product. Also make sure you are all on the same page about intended deliverables.

Step 3: Develop Your Project Plan

Again use the materials at
www.TheDigitalPLan.com/SitePlannningWorksheet

You start with the goals. Then add in the scoping to understand some broad ideas. Scoping should translate into building out a timetable with clear deliverables. I highly recommending having a clear plan that outlines a schedule for mockup review and web development review together in one place.

Make sure you know at each step who is accountable for the deliverables and who needs to review for sign-off. Here are some questions you'll need to answer.

> *Who is responsible for creating the mockup art for the page?*
> *Who is responsible for choosing or creating imagery for a page?*
> *Who is responsible for development of the page?*
> *Who must review the content before development?*
> *What is the timeline for that review?*
> *Who is the final decider on a mockup before production?*
> *Who all must review a page after development?*
> *What is the timeline for that review?*
> *Who is the final decider on a mockup before a page goes live?*

You should answer those questions in your plan. This should include all of your goals, benchmarks, and milestones. I highly recommend having all of this clearly laid out in your plan. If you are building a large multi-page site these questions will be even more invaluable. Personally I've watched projects get gridlocked on each of the questions above. If you get gridlocked in a few of those and things become unclear, I promise you a three month project will become five or six and a scramble to finish. A good plan won't avoid all of that either but will make it much better.

——TIP——

>In planning you should be sure to include a
>launch plan. I would make this a separate
>document from the detailed development plan.
>But a big mistake I've seen a few times is a lot of
>thoughtful development work with no launch plan.
>I'm going to assume if you are reading this, you
>are intending to have an impact no matter what
>your web development is.

This is the nuanced web that is digital. How do you intend to get people to engage with what you are developing? Is it paid ads, emails updates, earned media, social, media, or a combination? Good analytics can also help you track and plan where you get traffic.

Step 4: Execute project plan

Execution is fairly straightforward but my biggest tip is to be communicative. I highly recommend giving folks a weekly update on progress and where you might be ahead or behind.

——TIP——

>If you are doing a large in-house project that is
>going to suck up a lot of organizational capacity
>and don't have a pure project manager on staff, I
>recommend bringing in one if you can. On
>redeveloping the site for RAN.org, I often found
>myself holding some of that role and trading that
>off with others. That plus other day-to-day
>functions meant sending the weekly report would
>slip. It also meant the project pieces would
>sometimes live in limbo unclear of who had to
>drive which piece to completion.

You should be tracking your benchmarks and milestones. Update and evaluate as you go. I promise you, being behind rarely changes the deliverable dates in a linear way. That means being two days behind rarely just allows you to shift the deliverable date by two days or add capacity of 16 hours. It most likely means you've learned something about your plan and need to update the overall plan.

Step 5: Review Goals in Relation to the Executed Project. Learn.

Take time to review your top-level goals, benchmarks, and milestones. Are you meeting those goals? Are you getting the change in the world you wanted?

Some questions you should ask yourself in review and reflection:

> What did you learn in the day-to-day process? Did you learn anything in what is realistic in development for your organization? Are there elements of communication and approvals that could be improved?
>
> Are the actions happening the way you intended? Are things on the site functioning as you planned? If not, why not? If yes, is there anything you can carry forward into future projects?
>
> Are you getting the world impact you expected? If not, is it a problem of traffic and exposure? Did what you build work for your goals?

An important part of being able to answer these questions is having good analytics on your site. At the most basic level, make sure you have Google Analytics setup so you can at least understand site traffic. I highly recommend setting up the goal function of Google Analytics to know if the actions you intend are happening where you expect across the site.

Real Life Example -- Applying What You Learn

When we relaunched the website for RAN.org, we had planned everything on the homepage strategy. This design theory had two considerations: First, most websites of action and content based organizations don't get that much traffic to their homepage; it mostly comes through the action and content pages driven by social and email. Second, eliminating requests from staff and board members who couldn't find a particular thing on the homepage would eliminate repose and conversation time.

To our surprise, after the new site was live and we had a few months of valid data, we realized that 30% or so of our website traffic came through the homepage. This made sense given how much new traffic we were driving via earned media and ads. So we decided to rethink the goals of the homepage and how to be more intentional in delivering focused content that orientated new users to both active campaigns and the organization itself.

Summary

Once you know whether or not to start into a new web development project and if that is the best way to meet the goals, you are off to a well-framed start. It will help you answer which of the following kinds of projects you are digging into:
- For a new organization or campaign
- A new project
- Rebuilding an existing site

With those foundations laid, you can address questions about capacity and resources. With all of that answered, you can start to dig into the structural elements for web development and make sure it all meets your goals.

Email

Email is still king. Yes, even with the rise of social media, email is still the leader in engaging, tracking engagement, and empowering engagement.

Being such an important part of any program, we are going to use this section to dig deeply into how to think about email planning and theory. We'll go in-depth on structuring the right ask, to the right audience, at the right time. Email testing and structure are key to making the most of your program so we'll make sure you have the knowledge to make good decisions.

The best way to think about digital is as an ecosystem. To work at scale, a thriving ecosystem means planning for email, social, web development, graphic design, and video working together. Like any ecosystem if the major piece of the ecosystem is off, everything suffers or collapses. Email is often the lifeblood of a good digital ecosystem. If you want to be extremely effective, knowing ads and analytics will take you to that next level.

Email may be the best documented content stream in the digital space. This section will try to avoid rehashing the best practices you can find in other places and really aim to help you with practical email systems and planning.

One of the best places to get up to date with email best practices is from M+R Benchmarks and their writings throughout the year. The great reporting coming from NTEN.

Identifying Your Best Goal for Email

You've named your organizational or top project goal. The question should be: *How does email play a part in meeting that goal?*

Whether you are working on a project or a campaign, you need to know the overall goal and the milestone goals for phases. I laid out this theory in an online article by the same name of the theory called the Matrix of Engagement. (You can read it at www.TheDigitalPlan.com/MatrixOfEngagement). The biggest question to solve for in digital engagement is the right ask, to the right audience, at the right time. You have to know both your goals and something about your audience to know you can have a shot at making the right ask, to the right audience, at the right time.

Right Ask, Right Audience, Right Time

Strategic email planning for the Right Ask, is two fold: Does this ask link to the mission and end goal? If people engage in this ask, do they either move closer to an end goal or does the organization move closer?

Strategic email planning for the Right Ask, is two fold: First, make sure this ask links to the mission and what you have identified as organizational goals. Secondly, good planning should ensure when people engage in this ask, they either move closer to an end goal or the organization moves closer.

A bad email strategy would look like this:
Email ask >> Engagement >> only completes engagement disconnected from end goal

A good email strategy looks like this:
Email ask >> Engagement >> Action that gets closer to goal

Let's dive deeper. Can you clearly draw a line from the ask in an email to the end goal? If you answer, *yes, but...* for any one of these reasons:

We'll need to deeply explain to people how this ask contributes to our end goal.
We just think this is a good action to keep people engaged, but the direct connection is weak.
Well... it feels like a good action.
Yes we can but to date it hasn't had the impact we wanted on goals.

Then, you are closer to a *no* than a *yes*.

Good indicators of the right ask also develop over time.

————TIP————

> Build a tagging library. You'll see this again in
> Data and Analytics. But a tagging library should
> help you answer: Of the people on our list, who
> donates and how often? Who engages or has
> said they like which issues? How often do they
> engage, and what kinds of actions have they
> taken to date?

The indicators of the right ask are things like unsubscribe rate, list growth, increased engagement, and making the change you intend to have. Unsubscribes happen for a number of reasons and some have nothing to do with you such as overall email fatigue or change in passion, but most unsubscribes have everything to do with your planning. Unsubscribes can indicate things like whether or not the ask in the email felt disconnected from what they signed up for, that it may have been out of alignment with the values they believed they were aligning with, or they received more email volume than expected.

Real Life Example -- Asks and Unsubscribes

Working with a large organization, I believed that launching a monthly newsletter would drive more engagement across campaigns and build more organizational cohesion for supporters. But after a few attempts, the unsubscribes compared to the rate of people sharing it and expanding our list of supporters of one campaign joining another campaign, internally didn't balance out. We were burning off the list trying to get them more engaged. The newsletter was scuttled. It didn't solve for building what we intended and was an indicator we needed a new approach.

List growth from a good ask means you are delivering the kind of engagement people want. Not only are you delivering what people want but they feel compelled enough to engage and share it more widely. When you think of shares of content and actions, it isn't a mere tactical benefit, but an actual validation and benchmark for how much people are willing to endorse your organization.

Increased engagement from people on your email list over time is a prime indicator you are serving up the right kinds of asks. Make sure your email has some ability to look at the health of email open rates over time, actions based on type of action, and actions based on topics of interest.

Email Planning for the Right Audience

The right audience will be tricky and if you are just getting started or simply want to build good data on your email list, then the right audience could be everyone. However, more established organizations and building out good data rarely targets everyone. With good targeting and that specific right audience, you will be able to meet your end goal.

Some of the same indicators to determining the Right Ask, hold true here too such as unsubscribe rate, list growth, increased engagement etc. You'll want to know what is a good industry or niche average for things like open rates and unsubscribes to gauge if you are connecting to your list. I recommend starting with M+R's benchmarks because they have spent years building data sets from a number of fields on email. Then build data on your own to be able to benchmark how well you are connected to your audience on an email by email basis and over time.

The email templates I use in email planning all ask questions of topic, audience, and tactic because those question help think through the right ask, to the right audience, at the right time. To meet short term and long term goals it is important to be thoughtful on audience. Here are a few thoughts on how to choose audiences.

First, you need some data. If you don't have any, look at Data Library in the Data and Analytics section of the book and start building data. Every good email program uses data as its backbone.

Second, you'll need to know how large of an audience you need to meet your goal.

One way of determining this is by asking what type of impact your want the audience to drive. Here are a few examples:

Hosting an event:

I've seen a few examples of organizations want to ask everyone on their list to host an event. While that's not bad once in awhile, data is important because you can hurt overall engagement with a continued ask to the wrong audience. Are there any pieces of data you know about current hosts? Are there any typical actions they take? Are hosts more likely to be people who also attend events? Think about narrowing your audience best on ideas like that. Maybe simple things like first ask your previous hosts and then expanding audiences instead of driving unsubscribes from the bigger list.

Real Life Example -- Email Ask to a Specific Audience

Working on a project to eliminate rainforest tree pulp from a major fashion company's supply chain, we wanted to culture jam that corporation's hashtag by taking advantage of it. The plan was to use it to expose the labor issues in their supply chain related to that pulp. We could have asked everyone on our email list to join an action on Twitter, but we knew that Twitter use from the broader U.S. population isn't that high, and we didn't want to bombard a large group with several emails. We suspected based on past data on email unsubscribes that it may lead to a larger amount of unsubscribes than we were comfortable with. So we changed tactics and analyzed the corporation's hashtag. It looked like they received around 200 to 500 tweets a day on it, so we didn't need 500 to 1,000 tweets like we initially thought. We really just needed to get 100 to 250 tweets to gain the exposure we wanted.

So our main goal was to jam the hashtag. To meet that goal we had a benchmark of tweets we needed to be successful, so the audience we needed were likely people to join this twitter action. We backed out from the goal of a minimum of 100 unique tweets and we estimated an open rate of 15% and an action rate of 25% so we needed a list of 2,700. We took that 2,700 and asked ourselves: *do we think we have some audiences that would be right to ask to join this smaller targeted list?* Because we had been building data, we had a list of a few thousand people we thought we could convert a high percentage based on their past engagement with email action related to Twitter. We also then looked at a group of people we had tagged as interested in the issue and were also likely Twitter users. We emailed them to join our culture jam as well. What we ended up with, was the right audience that had opted into getting a series of emails over a few days. They had an average open rate of 30-40% with action rates over 40%. We reduced unsubscribes by targeting our audience according to high open and action rates because we knew these were indicators of the right audience getting the right ask at the right time.

The Value of a Subscriber

Building your audience should be about knowing your goals and what tradeoffs are worth. Let's say a fundraising deadline is looming. Your impulse may be to email everyone multiple times to ask for donations. An important piece of data you need to consider is the value of an email subscriber to your organization. You should use this number to help you answer whether or not expanding your audience is literally worth it in terms of potential unsubscribes.

Two easy questions to help determine the individual subscriber value to your organization include:
  1) What is the average email value?
  2) If you do paid email list building, how much do you pay per email per year?

If you send test emails (and yes you should always, always test - see section on Email Testing below) then you know the importance of finding the best option for compelling positive action. But you should also think about the cost. To dig into both questions a bit, here are some ways to think about it.

Email value per year is a simple equation of:

Total online fundraising in dollars ÷ Total number of emails on your list
= Average Email Value

In other words, if you raised $200k and had 50k emails on your list, your average value would be $4. So if you were setting an email intended to be a fundraiser, but had 500 people unsubscribe because of bad performance on the email, you lost the opportunity to raise a potential $2,000 from that list of emails that unsubscribed. If your goal was to raise $5,000 from the email send, but you lost $2,000 in potential annual revenue from the unsubscribes, your real net raised would only be $3,000. Now the individual email report wouldn't show that loss because most reporting only shows net raised. Knowing your organizational email value is highly important so you can better assess net cost and real amounts raised.

Paid email cost equation:

Total cost of new emails $\div$ Total number of emails you recruited = Cost per new email

In other words, if you spend $50k in ads to recruit 20k new emails to your list your cost per email is $2.50. If you are sending emails that lead to unsubscribes, is it worth the amount it will cost to get new emails back on the list? Let's say someone in the organization is pressuring you to send an email that performed poorly in tests, and it is likely to lead to 2,000 more unsubscribes. Knowing this value, you could ask them if it is literally worth $5,000 to send the email and, if yes, whose budget would pay to replace that many lost emails.

Email Planning for the Right Time

Right timing is mostly about two things: external factors and internal frequency. External factors include connecting the content to current issue-related calendars or broader external events in the world. Internal timing relates to the number and frequency of emails the organization sends.

Sometimes you have the right audience and right ask, but it comes at the wrong time. Bad timing can cost hours and dollars. Using the list cost above, and factoring staff time coming up short on plans, has real impact. On the fundraising side, I've participated in planning for multiple Earth Day emails that were executed at the right and wrong times. A few years back, there was a last minute rush to get a fundraising email out the door. If you considered yourself an environmentalist and subscribed to several email lists, then you probably received 5-20 fundraising asks that day. The email we sent probably came too late and maybe wasn't our prime day. A year later, we planned to send a fundraiser on a different day. We also decided to ask people to skip the easy donations and take action. It was successful, not just in engagement that day, but in broader engagement because supporters appreciated making the day about action.

Other external factors can be about what is happening broadly related to your issue or the world at large. Holiday weekends tend to be bad days to send emails. Most people are a little checked out from email during major holidays. But being able to sync your email up to breaking moments around your issue, or when your issue has mainstream press, almost always adds positive engagement.

Internal volume can have a big impact on email engagement. Do you consistently send three to four emails a week, or more like one to two every other week? A rapid increase from one a week to four can cause a lot of unsubscribes and might have less to do with the audience and more with the ask. Given the same asks to the same audience at expected time intervals that were more regular between you and your receiver, may have had better engagement and fewer unsubscribes.

Real Life Example -- Email and Timing

During my time at Organizing for Action, we had planned a day of action around yet another mass shooting because we wanted to pressure Congress on their continued inaction. Our broad goal was to get Congress to make a vote on some common sense reforms around access to firearms in the U.S. The tactical goal was to get a hashtag trending on Twitter because we wanted to create a national conversation and highlight the congresspeople who were still opposing sensible legislation. To do that, we built a number of benchmarks we intended to reach with internal accounts, partners, and supporters. We wanted these conversations to be as noticeable as possible to also attract press to help create a full feedback loop from Twitter to earned media and back to continued social media narrative highlighting representatives blocking legislation.

We emailed a much bigger audience to ask for tweets than I would normally recommend, knowing the overall lower rates of Twitter use compared to Facebook. We believed the theory of the ask and timing might appeal to a larger audience because we knew how passionate supporters were feeling at that time around gun violence reform. It was a success, trending all day, and gaining coverage across most major media outlets. Actually, it was so successful that many people created new twitter accounts that day just to speak out. One Representative in Texas received so many tweets, he accused us (and namely me) of using digital bots to attack him on Twitter. CNN validated that we just encouraged his constituents to create new accounts to message him. Had we sent such an ask weeks later or prior, I don't believe we would have had that kind of multi-step engagement. It was about making a higher bar ask at the right time.

Email testing: Always Be Testing

I once interviewed a candidate about how often they think it's necessary to perform subject line tests. They answered, *when there is time*. Wrong answer. Always test subject lines and performance before sending to a broad audience because every percentage point better in open and click rates is a literal shift in engaging thousands of people.

I've been asked a few times how small of a test is worth it. Some might say all sizes but I do think that 500 is probably the smallest test sample audience you'd want to send to. If you are in a planning phase or only have an email list of 2,000 people, then at the very least you could get a test of two subject lines to two groups of 500 people. Give it at least an hour or two and if the open rates are low, action rates are low, or unsubscribes are high, consider not sending the email.

Some Testing Scenarios Guidance

Sometimes folks ask what is the minimum number to test and what are some ways to think of list splits for tests. Here are some numbers I've found to be really helpful:

10,000 or fewer people
- Test three subject lines
- Create three groups of 1,000
- Send winning test to remaining 7,000.

100,000 people or more
You have some space here to be more creative. I would recommend at least
- Test three subject lines
- Create three groups of 3,000
- If one is performing great, send winner to remaining 91,000.
- If not, test two more subject lines each to groups of 3,000

If you are looking at 100,000 people or more I would also recommend some deeper testing like understanding if major cohorts in your emails perform differently. If you have two major tags you wanted to look at specific groups in, I would split this list to also test them.
- Test three subject lines
- Create three groups of 3,000 for cohort A
- Create three groups of 3,000 for cohort B
- Send winning test to remaining emails for cohort A
- Send winning test to remaining emails for cohort B

Splitting into further cohorts like that will allow you to learn more about how different groups respond to different kinds of asks and issues. That learning helps you better match the Right Ask, Right Audience, Right Time.

An important thing to remember is you can't test open rate (and sender name) or open rate content at the same time unless you have duplicates. For example, a non-valid test would be sending four different subject lines, but two from one sender and two from another. What would be valid is sending four tests, two subject lines from one sender and the exact same two from another sender. Use the same process if you want to test layout or content. Make sure the layout or content is the same from one sender to the other and they are getting the same subject line.

Always be testing! Testing two items in same test sample = bad test. Focus in on one test at a time.

We've got Right Ask, Right Audience, Right Time. And now you'll always be testing. Let's talk about email structure.

Strategic Email Structure

Every email is unique and the way you plan your email program will change the impact you have. Emails are most powerful when customized to the goal you need that email to achieve. An email can even have multiple goals, but you should avoid more than one ask. A split ask is when you give people two or more options in the email. Here, the paradox of choice kicks in. For every option you add, you decrease the likelihood that action will be taken on any option.

There are occasions where an email could have a split goal for impact. In addition to clear asks and good timing, emails are also about content theory. People start to think of the email audiences as falling into only one bucket like a donor, an in-person activist, or an online activist does. But part of good data is knowing the kinds of actions people will take. The split goal for impact could be both gaining event attendees and letting all subscribers know you are holding live events.

For example, let's say you have an upcoming series of events but the majority of people on your list have never attended an event before. Based on targeting audiences, some might be inclined to withhold a particular audience, such as donors, from the email. However, if hosting in-person events is key to your theory of change and it's important that people know the event is happening, email them all. In this case, the split goal is about both actual event attendance and wanting everyone to know you are fulfilling this part of your mission. You might be okay with a donor or two dropping off because building this narrative for everyone is important.

It's important to know your #1 goal for each email and make that the ask. Are you sending this email to drive online engagement, attend an event, make a donation, spread messaging, update supporters, or educate supporters?

Each of these different goals should actually have a somewhat different format to them. The format should help the reader focus on the intended impact because this is your ultimate goal. The following sections are some in-depth thoughts for specific formatting.

Email for Online Engagement or Calls

I would list in this category things like signing a petition, sending an email to a target, using social media to pressure a target, or make a phone call. These emails should be quick and to the point. You should assume that to some degree, people on your list are connected to your issue or theory of change. Good data can also confirm this to some extent.

Even if it's a new target or topic, but fits your campaign model, get to the action ask quickly and without getting entrenched in the story upfront. When your goal is action, focus on the action and make the execution of it as simple as possible. For example, if you are doing work around gun violence reform and you are driving a petition to a specific governor, then make the ask for a petition signature right up front. Don't spend sentences and paragraphs explaining gun violence or all the technical details of the bill, even if it is a governor you've never mentioned before in a state you haven't previously targeted. People have joined your email list because they trust you to determine if this tactic is the right one for this issue. Just get to the ask of signing and what it is for in the first two or three sentences.

Try to keep these kinds of emails to one to three short paragraphs. The only exception would be if you are making some complicated ask. Most asks like a petition take a minute or less to complete. A longer ask would be something you think requires several minutes of time rather than a minute or less form or quick phone call. Filling out a multistep comment form would be such an example. Tell people how long it will take and why it's important, and you'll see great results.

If you truly believe you need four to five paragraphs explaining an ask, I would question if you have the right audience. For most organizations that have done the work to build audience and trust two to three paragraphs is all you need for them to complete the ask.

Email for Fundraising

One of the most common email types across all organizations is a fundraising ask. Because of this, it is also probably the type of bad email we all see the most. Often, we get a laundry list of asks telling us why to give, or we get an update on everything the organization is doing. Sometimes these laundry lists of emails work and raise some funds, though people who give to these emails are most likely very deeply connected to your organization or issue.

Keep the email about the impact the donor is going to have on the issue. Make it appealing on an individual level. Try to keep it to one topic and, if you can, just one story. For example, one story may look like, lions are killed by poachers every day or so, but Cecil is one lion who stood out because people can personalize with one. Are you working on a water crisis in the U.S. or abroad? Include a fact or two to support your cause but don't give people painful facts to make your case. Give them the human story of one human impacted by the water issue, and let them put themselves in that person's shoes to allow them to be an agent of positive change in the story.

Most humans relate to stories better than numbers, so use facts and statistics sparingly to validate your story. Yes, issue campaigners are often a treasure trove of facts and statistics. Use those in informational documents. Use a good story and one direct ask to fundraise.

Email for Events

Keep it about the event, plain and simple. If you need to educate people on the event and issue, you probably have the wrong audience.

Make it timely. For some major events, long-term notice is ok. Otherwise, keep it no more than two weeks out unless it's something people have to book travel for.

Emails like this are typically best formatted as a few sentences about what you are doing. Event details and sign-up are all you need. And if you want, add a paragraph or two of what will happen at the event.

Did I forget important facts and statistics on the issue? No, they don't belong here. I am harping on this because so many organizations litter their content with overkill information that distracts people from taking the goal action.

Email to Spread Messaging

This is another simple type of email tactic. Did your organization get awesome press, release a new document in the world, or have a messaging narrative you want to drive via social media? Make it short and summarize why that piece of content is important, not the issue. You should be sending this to people already vested in the organization or issue.

Write a sentence or two and share. Maybe a paragraph on why sharing is important to your theory of change and why the reader taking action makes an impact.

That's it.

Email to Update or Educate Supporters

This is your chance to be wonky. Don't confuse this with taking an action or making a donation. If you want to put an ask at the end, that's great, but if the ask at the end is your goal, and you married it under paragraphs of text, you'll probably miss your goal.

These are the kinds of emails where you can breakdown facts and give some story to statistics. I personally think many people want more of these from organizations separated from other asks. Most people are interested to know more about things they care for. I also believe delivering a few of these over the year can and should have a net positive impact on other actions like petitions, attending events and donating.

Email Planning Guidance

We've covered Right Ask, Right Audience, Right Time. You now know to always be testing. You've got email structure ideas to play with and now, let's plan it all out.

Email planning should be about building a good system in your project or organization to get great content planned, approved, and out to supporters. To make this happen I think it's important to have these items in place: a calendar, layout and approval checks, data and tagging systems, and review and feedback mechanisms.

<u>Email Calendar</u>

Keep it simple and make it part of your internal calendaring system. Personally, I love using a Google calendar if possible. Create a calendar event for the day it's going out. Include the topic and audience.

In your project space, the minute you have a possible date, add it to your calendar with the intended audience identified. Adding the intended audience always makes it easier to know if an email should be moved a day or not. Were you planning on launching two petitions to an overlapping group? Probably a bad idea because it feels like you are asking a lot in one day. Were you planning on a petition email and an ask to attend a cool local event in one city? It could be okay for someone to get two emails from you the same day if they are added value. If the petition was for an issue someone cared about, followed by an invite to an event hours later, there is likely to be a positive impact to attendance because you'll be fresh in their minds.

Keep what is rapid response rapid, and plan the rest. One of the biggest struggles I've seen in scaling a good email program, is the burden of time when rushed. If a few people need to review an email, give them time to schedule themselves around other work and you'll most likely get a better product than pushing for a last minute review.

Email Drafting Layout and Approval Checks

Clearly, the approval checks have a calendar component and it links in well with drafting layout. Make it easy for people to get a good sense of the email content by using a consistent drafting and editing system.

I recommend using a Google doc or other shared online document system because they allow for notes and redrafts in the same place. You should include things like audience, email goal, and subject lines all in the drafting document.

Personally. I also like to include landing page text in the same document if there is any reason for a new action or donation page.

When it comes to approvals, I recommend trying to get a system of no more than three or four people that have full sign-off power. Maybe you include someone else for fact checking, but keep it to who must say yes or no. In my current role as digital director, I don't sign-off on every email. I believe that we hired quality people to create content for the organization so as long as it's been seen by someone with communications and campaign authority on that topic, it's good. I try to review as many as I can, but I work more with my team in looking at trends and performance than grammar editing.

Email Data and Tagging Systems

I've mentioned much about tagging. I speak from painful experience where I inherited an email program that had three main tags. We had no clue what kinds of actions people were taking or how often. That made it hard to really know who was on the email list and how to get the right asks to people. Most email clients currently have some ability to tag people. I say work with what you have but if you are planning to scale, make sure your system can hold good data over time.

Email Review and Learn

Clearly you need data for this. I would encourage you to also make sure you can look at past emails and performance. I would recommend a spreadsheet that has the type of email as well as information about email content performance like open rates, test sizes, unsubscribes, spam rates, and any other metric that helps you learn how to better serve your audience.

I would also encourage you to make it easy to review content. In one role, I had to use NationBuilder, which isn't great for searching for old emails by send. So we forward the winning email plus stats on tests to an emailreport@emailaddress to build an archive with a good date range. It's invaluable to look at real data with real content instead of making guesses about last year.

Use benchmarks for the amount of emails you want to send, and track benchmarks for kinds of emails and outcomes. That kind of knowledge will help you match the Right Ask, to the Right Audience, at the Right Time.

Email Expectations

Not knowing the goals the impact for each email will lead to overall less impact.

But less is actually more in regards to stats and facts around issues when the ask is simple. That kind of less will get more impact by not overwhelming the reader.

Email is not a silver bullet to anything. It won't save your messaging problem if you have bad messaging. Or fundraising if you have bad asks. But when you work through good planning around the right ask, to the right audience, at the right time you have the ability to leverage the most effective engagement medium (literally) at your fingertips. That is why email is still king and, done well, it has the ability to change strategic impact across all organizational goals.

Design

Strategic design is fundamental to communication and engagement. Yet, again and again, I see design being the underfunded and unplanned part of projects, organizations, and campaigns. We are going to dig into why you need to be strategic with planning and funding good design, and then how to plan for it.

Good design crosses all platforms and mediums. It gives an emotional element to your work that shifts your appeal from just an issue or a person to a feeling. Humans are more powerfully moved by feelings than facts. If you can combine compelling facts and reason with design that is appealing, you'll have more compelling content with a level of engagement that can help lead to major wins.

This chapter will break down design into a few sections:
A Case for Design Investment
How to Plan Strategic Design
Feelings for Design
Design for Logos and Branding Plans
Design for Website Planning
Design for Social Planning
Design for Print Planning

Story: Great Design Works

When I accepted the role at RAN (Rainforest Action Network) one of my biggest concerns was design capacity and making the budget case for a talented graphic designer. I've seen a number of organizations think of design as *a nice thing to have*, instead of *a must have* when it comes to capacity and budget. I believe it comes from a misunderstanding about what moves people and the true impact of design in connecting with people by inciting emotions and feelings.

I had the pleasure of working with very talented designers and design teams at all of the Obama organizations I worked with.

Working with talented designers, it was powerful to see the impact of proper design to make content engaging, and often more clear, either in simplicity or legibility. Those designers would take rough mock up ideas campaigners presented them with, and they engaged in the art side of digital for impact. On the flip side, I've seen a number of campaigns and NGOs expect design to be voluntary or just a thing someone with Photoshop can do. There are a lot of skillful self-taught designers out there, but just having a design tool doesn't make someone a designer any more than buying a stethoscope makes me a Doctor.

I was delighted when I found out we not only had a Senior Art Director who focused mostly on print, special event design, and overall brand design management, but we also had an in-house designer, Jake Conroy, focused on website and social media design. But because of some unclear planning, his designs weren't being consistently used on social media. The Facebook page was in moderate shape with 80k likes. By employing consistent content design that allowed a very talented designer to do what he does best, the page started on a trajectory of sharp growth in likes and engagement. We mixed his good design with consistency in frequency, timing, and quality of content. Within a few months, we rushed passed 100k likes - a growth rate of 25%. Empowering the designer to drive smart and engaging design, we saw a number of posts getting hundreds of thousands of impressions converting into new fans, which meant more people signing petitions, taking actions, and connecting with the organization. Over the following year, the page tripled in size, much of that growth directly attributable to good and consistent design.

A Case for Design Investment

Good design is essential to good campaigning. As noted above, design empowers communication and engagement, two of the most fundamental building blocks of digital strategy. But in a world with tight resources, it is understandable you might find yourself needing to make the case for investing in design. I know I have, so let's walk through some tangible value to design.

Here are a few of the direct values of good design:

Consistent design reinforces your brand and builds the connection to your organization, campaign, or cause. Think about the Obama O, the Hillary H, World Wildlife Fund's panda, or the Twitter bird. Their consistent design from branding to content builds relationships with their audiences.

Good design makes your content engaging. If you intended to engage people in your cause or campaign, this investment will go a long way. This is exactly why major companies will spend millions of dollars on a single design campaign.

Good design creates value you can get a return on. There is multistep and direct return.

Multistep return would be when good design increases Facebook engagement. Increased Facebook engagement leads to more signatures on a petition. You then receive a direct organizational value when those emails later convert to donors.

Direct return comes when you invest in good design for images placed in emails. I've seen well-designed images in fundraising emails perform between 10-30% better than emails without well-designed images.

How to Plan Design

Planning good design gets back to knowing your goals. What exactly is your goal and intended impact?

The best design comes with parameters. Not all design needs to be out-of-the-box. The best brainstorms and creations happen with clear guidelines. Designing for effective campaigning is all about achieving goals.

The best parameters also define scope, which is a way of asking - what exactly do you need?

You should be able to identify the medium, volume, audience, and ultimately the impact you need from a piece of design.

Medium: Here we are defining medium as a channel of communication. This could be a really wide range of things like print for a billboard, trifold handout, or black and white flyer. Design for a social media platform has specific sizing parameters. Website design could include an image for a feature area, image in a blog or email, or even a full page. Medium is important because it creates a good initial guide for choosing size, space, color, the complexity of the graphic, and the written content.

Volume: This is the variance in design production you need. If you need a design to appear on just a flyer, that is a very different project than if you want a similar feel on a piece of content that appears on a billboard, video, blog, and flyers. It could also be volume of related pieces like having 10 social media images for a new campaign. Volume changes planning and capacity a lot. You should make sure the volume matches the goals of the campaign.

Audience: This is whom you intend to engage. Different groups of people respond to design in different ways because of personal and cultural taste preferences. There really isn't 'good' universal design because it is inherently subjective. What can feel old and stale to one group could feel comfortable and assuring to another. There are a few ways to approach designing for communities. Approach one, is working with a designer that is from the community you intend to reach. The other is research and understanding what contemporary design looks like on online channels and other mediums that resonate with your audience.

On a deeper design level, if you want to be powerfully engaging, you should be able to talk about the feeling and characteristics of the design. The feelings and characteristics you want the design to have should directly portray the feelings you want it to evoke. For example, if you want your message to be *strong* you may consider using hard angles as opposed to more curved edges that often get portrayed as soft. Being able to portray feelings that clearly represent your message is a great way to efficiently expedite good design.

Feelings of Design

Working on the National Day of Service - a combined event as part of the Obama Presidential Inauguration and service in honor of Dr. Martin Luther King - I had the honor of working to facilitate the brand design. I worked with the team planning the overall events along with the in-house designer. We went through several rounds of iterative design because of mixed ideas about the feeling of what we needed.

Our first draft felt rustic and classic. The designer and I kicked around some ideas and she designed fantastic mockups, pulling from vintage gasoline company sign designs. These were designs people knew and had seen portrayed in classic events. She added in some texture to make it look weathered and classic.

In review, folks "liked" the designs but it wasn't quite what they asked for. The reality is they hadn't really dug into what they were actually asking for and were describing surface feelings without any depth. They had imagined some of the depth already but didn't express it. We were able to then get deeper descriptions of more institutional classic feelings like something that might fit within the categories of retro pentagon, boy and girl scout merit badges or National Park feelings.

Now we were cooking. The designer and I kicked around a few ideas to see if we were distilling the same ideas from what we were hearing. The luxury of a good designer is someone who can listen and turn what is heard into feelings evolved by their design. What we came back with was a few options that were, in reality, easy to sort through. Combining some final elements, we were able to move forward with the brand and subsequent materials.

With a broader overview and some of the right questions to ask on design, let's dig in on a few tips for specific kinds of projects. One overarching tip to keep in mind is that design is subjective. Being clear about parameters and expected outcomes will get you to an ideal outcome faster.

Design for Logos and Brand Planning Tips

Logo and brand identity are key to overall organizational communication. They should (over time) reinforce who you are, what you do, and tell a micro story. Logos and design tell this micro story by drawing on feelings and identities to related organizations or projects and the connection people have to your work. This micro story is a segue and an element of the start of all communication from your brand. Here are a few ways to think about brand identity to make sure your design meets your goals.

Designing for logos and branding can be crucial to the life of a project, organization, or campaign. One important thing to remember is designs can evolve. While I wouldn't recommend constantly going through major overhauls, if you are just getting started, don't feel like what you start with is the final iteration. Establish a design that conveys what you want and let it evolve as people interact with you.

Be clear on your scope and the outcome of what you need and can afford. Working with clients and designers, I am always careful to be real about the amount of revisions expected and the complexity for which we have time or budget. Each revision is costing you direct funds paid to design teams as well as organizational time, taking away from work on other projects. I've worked on projects where we were clear that with a particular deadline and budget, we could do stylized font plus a predetermined shape. It is all about matching up the resources available to the goals.

Be clear on how you want your project portrayed. Establish how you want to be viewed by people who will be supporters and those you wish to influence. Are you a young upstart or are you a modern and strong institution? At the end of the day if you don't define it, someone else will. A style guide is a simple document that helps make sure everyone involved is part of building brand consistency.

A complete style guide should have the following:
- Guidance on how to use and place the logo.
- Organizational fonts for logo, organizational name, print and online text.

- Organizational color palette.
- Alternate use colors for logo if needed for black and white and simplified use for stencils

Take time to establish the right feelings and make sure your brand resonates with people the way you intended it to. Then make sure you build out a style guide for brand consistency.

Design for Website Planning Tips

Website design is a robust and often complicated process. Websites for campaigns, nonprofits, and activism projects are often part storytelling, part action, part resource center, and part information for various audiences. The sheer scale of complication of all those pieces means you should treat your design process with the diligence it needs to meet your goals. Here are a few more tips for success.

Know what you are trying to design. Is it a full website or a page or feature? Be sure to select a designer that has worked with a project of the scope you need. The exception would be if you were willing to go through the time and process for someone to learn during the build.

Make sure you have designs that work for desktop, mobile, and tablets.

Make sure the designs work in a functional way.

Look at other websites you admire and, in the design process, ask a developer how complicated and expensive features you like are. It's kind of like pointing at a Tesla and saying you want that when you have the budget for an electric scooter. Good planning makes sure you align realistic outcomes with your budget.

Design for Social Media Planning Tips

Great social media often includes great design. There are certainly outliers of accounts that get by with minimal design, but those are the exception. Most engaging accounts take the visual medium seriously and so should you. Make sure you are planning out social media in a way that meets organizational goals but doesn't sacrifice one time asks for long term engagement. Here are tips for the planning process.

Make sure you know the platform and where it is going. A Facebook event image is different than an image you want to autoload for a blog and it is also different from a share graphic.

Test. Social is a great place to test what resonates. Track your social content over time and use that to influence your design.

Let images be images. I mean, don't try to cram every word onto an image. Yes, sometimes you see an "image" that is just text. Rarely do those outperform simple text and compelling images.

Use images to lead and be honest about what comes next. People don't like clickbait. Let an image be real about what they will find from your report, action, or article.

Reuse. Yes, people will likely engage again with your content even if they've seen it before. Repetitive branding is even good.

Keep your social media design authentic to your overall brand and messaging.

Design for Print Planning Tips

My experience over the years is that print designing, while it used to be the staple, is less common for most of us in the campaigns and nonprofit space because of the rise of digital. I'm including it here because it comes up as an ask for most graphic designers. The reality is, most designs that work great for the internet don't translate perfectly to print items like T-Shirts, flyers, and posters. So make sure you plan well for these separately if they are part of your goals.

Really, really know your specifications here. I've watched a number of folks feel good about design and have it look and read horrible once printed.

If this is a new space for you or the designer you are working with, lean on templates. Getting the print margins or look of a large sign correct is rarely easy.

If you are working with a print shop, ask them upfront for all the print specifications.

Summary

Strategic design is essential for communication and engagement. Knowing the parameters medium, volume, and audience you need to design for will help make sure you meet your goals. Using those parameters as guidelines you can make be certain to use resources well and make an impact in the world.

Video

Video, possibly more than any other medium is consistently confused for the goal when it is more accurately a tactic and a medium. For Example, "make a viral video" is not a goal.

Whew... got that out of the way.

What is the goal of the video you intend to make? In this section, I will break down some of the questions around goals because increasingly, videos are accessible and made by lots of people. That doesn't mean they should be made by just anyone with your logo on it. This chapter will outline the elements that help you to resourcefully produce a high-quality video.

If your goal is to educate, raise awareness, inspire, raise engagement, or build brand identity, these could be good goals for a video. More than other very intensive digital tactics, video can be hard to measure for concrete goals other than views. Yes, you can measure post view impacts, but getting views first takes strategy. Even having one of the goals above doesn't always mean the investment in video is a good idea. Video is a great investment when you've made a decision on the tradeoffs between making a great video and other forms of content. Making sure video is a conscious and well thought out decision is the best way to meet any goal.

Where I would highly caution against video is when you want it as a means to quickly reach another goal directly. For example, if you want video to increase signups for one activity, donate right now, take an action right now, then it probably isn't the best tactic. There is overwhelming science behind low rates of watching a video to its end, and even lower post viewing action rates. But if you see video as a step of engagement to impact goals, that is a viable strategy. Video is about storytelling and persuasion, and if your goal is to connect deeply with your audience, then it is a tactic worth investing in. I'll expand more on this below.

This chapter is broken down into a few sections:

Video with View-Based Goals
Tips on Making Video Work
Video to Impact Other Goals
Video Launch Plan: Goals and Tips
Video Planning: Production Tips

Video with View-Based Goals

You have a goal and it is to educate, raise awareness, inspire, raise engagement, or build brand identity. The first two questions should always be: Is video the right medium? And, do we believe we are equipped to achieve the reach we want?

Is video the right medium for achieving your goal? If you are trying to raise awareness or education on a topic, could this be better achieved through a series of blog posts? Could it be achieved through a series of social media share graphics instead of one longer video? Could it be achieved with a content rich special page or website? Quite often people want to leap to video because it is a familiar medium most of us grew up with and are immersed in daily. But the ubiquitous nature of video doesn't mean it is always the best way to educate when you consider the many aspects of video. For example, if audio is important to the video working, you are really limiting the audience to when they have the freedom to listen to the video.

Don't rush to reject other content mediums because you want a video. Video requires a large investment of resources so you want to make sure you're intentional with your goal for using video as a tactic. Look at your video view rates vs. overall content consumption rates. Which is more likely to move the needle for you to help you reach your end goal?

Another aspect to consider is whether or not you are equipped to get the reach you want. I'll expand more below in launch plans, but essentially you want to ask: do you have an audience now or do you need to build one to get the views you need? Think about your email and social media reach and average engagement. If email and social media are the video distribution avenues that you are working with, then consider that many videos only achieve 30 seconds of views via social media. Do you have the infrastructure of reach already in place to have the impact you hoped for? There is a major difference in hoping and planning for success. Knowing the target you need to hit and figuring out how to hit it, is what a plan with good strategy should do.

If it isn't social media and email alone, you should think about the budget needed to get views via online ads. Other strategies could and should include using allies and people connected to your organization with their own social media and email reach that would also drive the video. Don't let your email list size and social media reach be the block if you have good content that drives important goals. You should leverage all of your reach to get it out there.

If you don't currently have the audience to drive the views, but you want to create a video that will serve as background content on an issue for the next twelve months, that is a good use of video. You have a clear intention for the video and feel good about the long-term investment that it doesn't matter you aren't going to get the views you need now. An informational video is a great way to give your content a longer life span.

I love video and think most organizations can invest in it differently. Using video as a piece of well-planned messaging in an Ecosystem of Content, you'll find there are many, many good uses for video. Good video engages in storytelling, it follows formats and formulas, and it is clear about message of both story and action.

Tips on Making Video Work

Outlined below are video planning tips for using video to educate, raise awareness, inspire, raise engagement, or build brand identity. If you are intending to shift behavior, you should either be following a storyline arc or a clear explanation arc. There are volumes and volumes of work on creating good storytelling videos. Here are some of my favorite elements to consider:

Agreement
Context— Problem/pain and vision of solution

Story
Connection
Description
Realization of solution—how
Call to action

If you need to create explanation videos, I highly recommend picking up the book, *The Art of Explanation*. It is made by the creators of Common Craft videos. If you are new to video, don't just say "Ah! I get it." Just pick up a copy of their book and I promise every video and piece of content you make thereafter will be better.

Good videos can orientate a person to an issue and give them a connection to either the problem or the solution makers. It's not easy to track if an action successfully follows a video view since there are usually multiple paths that lead to an end goal. For this reason, you can either think about video as valuable for brand building and identity connection, or you can carefully time the release of the video to see if it creates a surge in actions toward an end goal.

If you have the capacity to invest in video, think of it beyond an immediate return. When a video consistently appears, even for a few seconds in your followers' Facebook and Twitter timelines, then you are building a narrative. That narrative should be around the work you engage in. Even if someone isn't watching to completion, it might be enough to continue to keep your organization front of mind for people.

And now for your video tips!

Tip 1: Know your goal and target audience. Goal should be simple like we need to share the story of x community or we want supporters to get a consistent update from our Executive Director.

Audience: It's best to pick just one. When you try to appeal to too many audiences, your message gets lost. You should be able to say we are appealing to current supporters, potential new supporters, a particular target group, or an entirely new audience. It's best to be specific.

Tip 2: Be real about your intended impact of each video. Don't imagine this is going to be "viral," because that would mean your video is being shared to new audiences that you don't normally interact with. Those are audiences you probably aren't the most informed on, making it hard to predict success.

Tip 3: Pay the proper cost. Quality video can be expensive. A short two-minute to five-minute piece done by a professional firm can cost $5,000 for some basic work. It's likely to cost north of $20,000 if it involves animation, a lot of interviews, or filming on different locations. Those are fair rates for talented professionals. You can find cheaper and you should make sure what you see in a contractor's reel is what you want.

Tip 4: Stop over-analyzing the transition or exact sound at a certain moment. If you aren't a videographer then trust them. The biggest impact you can make depends on big picture message and feel. If you are obsessing over little things, you are probably off track.

Tip 5: Audio, audio, audio. If you are trying to do in-house video, invest in audio gear. If you have good audio, you can always add static images or graphics behind it. There's very little that a video editor can do for bad audio. High quality voiceovers can go a long way.

Tip 6: Think about the cuts. If you are investing in one larger video, can you also make shorter cuts to add quality volume to social media? The answer is usually, yes.

Tip 7: Lighting. You don't need an expensive kit but just knowing the basics of good lighting will take a modest video to a more professional level.

Video as a Means to Impact Other Goals

Imagine your goal is to get immediate sign-ups for an event. You or someone in your organization deeply believes that a video is what will do the trick. I've been down this road several times in the multiple Obama related organizations, and at RAN. To date, the data has always pointed to the video decreasing net sign-ups. The reason is similar to the paradox of choice: having to make a decision on either thing also makes you more likely to do neither thing.

Think about it this way - you want to get someone to a piece of content so they can watch all of that content. Then you want them to take a direct action like donate, sign up for an event, or maybe commit to a longer form of volunteering. Your intuition tells you that more information is more likely to get them to sign-up. I get it - on an intuitive level it makes sense, but to date I have yet to see it bear that kind of fruit.

In several cases, it does make strategic sense to pursue video to impact other engagement goals. These instances would be when it isn't the primary or only way to meet the goal but you are using video as a piece (or pieces) of content in a broader Ecosystem of Content. Times when this makes sense include:

- You have an abundance of capital for the project and you can layer in video.
- You have an abundance of video production capacity.
- The goal is not possible to meet with email and direct social media asks alone, so you layer in video as supplemental content.

Let's dig into the latter, layering in video as supplemental content. Whatever the main ask is that you need to convert on, make sure you have built simple pages that make it easy to convert to that ask from email and social. If you know preemptively that you'll never get the conversions you need, then you should be thinking about how to engage people more broadly and this is where video fits in.

Here is where it would make sense to develop engaging video content as a supplemental ask. Very specifically, you would use the video as an engagement hook and link to that action you need conversions on. You could even build out a secondary action page that includes video and an action. Don't make that combined action and video page your main push because, as described above, the paradox of choice will almost always suppress both. Make it a piece of a broader push to build out a full Ecosystem of Content around the action, and one of many ways people can connect to the action. Using video to impact another goal in that way is strategic and will help get you the conversions you are looking for.

Real Life Example -- Videos Register Voters

One project I worked on where video made sense to drive a specific goal was for voter registration in Nevada during the Obama 2012 campaign. We had a staggeringly large voter registration goal and we had the amazing luxury of online voter registration. A place where tweets and video links to registration makes a very real difference.

We had in-house video capacity because we were lucky to have recruited Tiffani Davis to come out and join us and we had strong statistics on how many voters per hour someone registered. Based on past experience, we estimated three in-person registrations an hour. It's hard to do voter registration for more than a few hours, so a single person might be able to get 10 to 12 registrations before tiring. So we broke down the numbers and realized if we got 3,000 or more views on a video, we felt confident it may translate to 30 registrations (at an estimated rate of 1% conversion to registration). We had the social media means and some noteworthy spokespeople in the state available to us, and we knew if we could turnaround two videos a week with that as the baseline goal, then we could reach people in a way we wouldn't otherwise. Video as a tactic made sense, because it was a piece of content in a broad ecosystem. There would be a volley of tweets, blogs, Facebook, posts, and apps driving registration.

Given the power of shifting the electorate and knowing that we were peaking on the number of people we could register in-person with our resources, video made sense. We were able to identify our goal, audience, and intended outcome, and the clarity of all drove our success.

Video Launch Plan: Goals and Tips

Now that you have some tips on video production for advocacy at large, let's talk about a launch plan. I've actually been part of a few projects where a video that was reasonably expensive got green lit in one department without figuring out a launch plan.

A launch plan is about how you are going to get views on the video, and it needs to start with the goal of the video.

Know your intended audience because the video should be all about you reaching them. If the rest of the plan doesn't add up to you reaching that audience, you don't have a strategic plan, plain and simple.

So you know your goal and your intended audience. Now you should know how many people you intend to impact with the video. If you can't answer with a target impact, you probably shouldn't be making the video or pushing for it until you can. Know the impact you want to make and you are on the right track to creating and launching a successful video.

Real Life Example -- Video Audience

At Rainforest Action Network, an idea came up to develop a video that was orientated around a few major donors of the Executive Director giving an update. The idea was pitched to me with hesitancy. Most of the hesitation was coming from the idea it may be an overuse of resources for a small target.

I suggested we create a plan for a video that focused on two overlapping audiences with the major donors as a subset of general supporters. I don't think this video will get a massive amount of views but we were at a point where developing more organization-wide narrative beyond just the campaigns, was a priority. We believed engaging more people as supporters, of not just individual campaigns, but supporters of the organization, would make it easier to transition more people to new campaigns and give us increased capacity over time. But if this video were part of an ongoing series shot in a simple yet compelling way, we could move people in increments. This made sense because I believe being thoughtful about Content in the Ecosystem makes it easier to move people through the Matrix of Engagement.

Being thoughtful in this case meant shooting for 4,000 views across platforms with about 1,000 people getting to the end.

Because if we can incrementally move 1,000 people at a time to be committed to the organization's systemic theory of change, we have the ability get a real impact in action, support, and fundraising.

Methods for Generating Views

With audience and intended impact laid out, you can now focus on how you are going to get the views. This is the crucial piece for making the impact you want with video. Think through the channels you have and what the views might be worth for you.

Here is a breakdown of the different channels, their value, and effort.

Social Media

Social media channels and algorithms currently thrive on video. In this space, it is a question of how much video you can feed it. However, if you don't have active social media channels, you can't bank much here. Take a look at engagement you've had around other content and try to approximate the amount of engagement you might have in the future. Good video often performs as well or better than great images on Facebook and Twitter. Instagram can be a bit harder to gauge image vs. video. Also consider longevity: does the video have a short shelf life, meaning it is only relevant for a few days, for a few weeks, or is it evergreen?

If it is relevant over a longer period of time, you should have a plan that lays out when you'll be posting it over time. If it is a short period, really focus in on your optimal time slots. And if the views are critical, even consider an extra post or two beyond your normal good rate. Meaning, if you normally get 2,000 views on a post and you think posting this video a third time will bring your average down to 400 views, it might be worth it if you have a goal focused on shifting outcomes.

Email

Email and video planning can be tricky. If it's a big video with important production value, it makes sense to email but to what impact? Is your email audience your target audience? If not, you should decide if your email list impacts your target audience by sharing it with them or helping raise public discourse around the video.

Two ways to think of measuring the impact on your target audience are in terms of viewer and number of views. Being a viewer is simple - you need to get your target audience's eyeballs on the video. Number of views is another soft form of impact. Let's say you have a political or corporate target that you think can be influenced by knowing your video got a lot of views. In this case, it might not be about exact quality of views, but total number of views plus getting to your target.

Good email list segmentation and tagging are important because they help you target your content to the right audience. Consider whether you'd like to generate a view or a share. I know it might seem intuitive that if people watch the video, they will share it, but just think about how many videos you see that you don't share. People are more likely to share a video when asked. Deciding which is more important will help you make the right ask to the right audience to watch or to share. You may have different segments from your list with which you can target different calls to action. Perhaps one group you want to target for watching and one for sharing. That's ideal, because it means you are making very intentional decision on audience types and the impacts you want.

Lastly on email, know what it is worth for you to get views. As in, what level of email unsubscribes are you willing to withstand for sending the video? It is a question you should ask on all emails. Paid email acquisition rates average $1-5 per email address for most political and nonprofits. Then consider that the statistics that come from M+R every year show most nonprofits average $1-10 per email. What could your costs in unsubscribes be if you are reaching the wrong audience on your email list? It's good to know your cost per email address for your organization and balance that with getting views via organic or paid social media promotion.

Website

Many people imagine that, when they put a video on their site, people will just come watch. Well if you look at many organizations' YouTube stats on videos on pages, you'll probably see they are low. The reality for organizations for whom media isn't their main focus, means the website is rarely the consumption point of video viewing unless driven there by email, social, press, or ads.

I think you should put all relevant videos on your site, just don't expect a lot of views to just happen on the site. The views you get there are more likely to be of high organizational value. Someone coming to your site and engaging in a lot of content builds a higher likelihood for long-term engagement.

Online Ads

Here is where getting the audience you want is truly up to you and your budget. Knowing your intended audience on a granular level can have huge impact. You can refine by many key factors, even making sure people on your email list see it. Make sure you know what you are doing or work with an ads consultant before you just "boost" the video to get a lot of random views.

Partners and Celebrities

How are you thinking about engaging partners to ask them to share it? Is it a good email ask for them? Would it make an easy ask for social media?

Same for celebrities or people that carry some social clout in the audience you want to reach.

Earned Media

Creating a video that has a press-worthy angle should be thoughtful. Why is it press-worthy? Are you exposing something new? Expressing a new angle? You should be able to think through what kind of success you've had before with press and determine to what level you think there may be additive views. Maybe not just from broadcast or online media, but also niche online publications and blogs.

Video Planning: Production Tips

If you haven't spent a lot of time in video, here are a few tips to help you make a video more productive and your work with a video firm much easier.

#1 Create a script or outline
Make sure you have a basic working script and at least an outline of how the shots will work together. What are the things you need to have said and imagery you need?

#2 Shoot only what you need
This is very informed by #1. Often folks think I will just shoot some stuff and we'll edit it down. I personally worked as a freelance videographer for about a year. The biggest early mistake I made was shooting too much. Why would I want to review four hours of video to cut down to a few minutes?

#3 Keep it simple.
Keep it truly simple, simple. Are you making a quick DTC (Direct to Camera) from a supporter or staffer? Don't try to add in a bunch of funky cuts and edits. Just keep it to the core content. And even on the longer pieces, don't rely on a lot of fancy cuts and text moving. Only caveat there being, if you are doing a full video or full sections of motion graphics or animations.

#4 Live events are hard
Whether you are hoping to get shots from a live event or cover something live, remember it's hard to get the exact or compelling shots. Make a shot list. This goes back to have a script or outline. That should help you be in position to get the right shots at the right time.

Going truly live is a different beast. My best recommendation is either be ready for something very unscripted or have your viewers wait through some awkwardness. I've personally had very mixed results and, to date, have yet to have an experience where I would say going live was better than having at least a few seconds to a few minutes to share great clips on social.

While on the Obama campaign, we experimented with live using the Google+ YouTube Live tool. A campaign surrogate went very,

very off message while we were live. Needless to say that was the last impromptu livestream I suggested for the cycle.

#5 Audio
From tips above, audio is so crucial. Make sure you plan to have that good audio. How will you get the sounds you need? Editing audio without expensive high quality software and equipment is rarely easy.

#6 Lighting and background
Take some time and plan where you will shoot. Especially if you are planning to do something simple in an office. Can you declutter the background? Then make sure the lighting will work. Make sure there isn't some awkward overhead or side lighting you can't control.

Social Media

Where to even start? Most advice I've seen is wrong on a platform by platform basis, because the advice is almost absent of connecting it to goals and impact. I guess let's start with, it is not free. At the very least it takes an investment in staff time and that is a cost. Done well and at scale, social media can be fairly expensive and yet there has never been a better way to have consistent engagement with supporters than social media.

The Matrix of Engagement, similar to the ladder of engagement, is about how you make a proactive ask and manage supporters. If the Matrix of Engagement is how you think about the ask and engagement of supporters, then the companion theory to that would be an Ecosystem of Content. Basically everything you use to engage users is content. Tweets, meta tags, subject lines, videos, URL names, Facebook descriptions, are all kinds of content. Social media is one of the most rapid and evolving spaces for real-time, content-based engagement.

There is no one-size-fits-all social media plan or growth plan. I firmly believe anyone that tries to tell you that is a hack. Just like every section of the book, the main question here is what is your goal? Social media is not one thing. Social media is a series of different content platforms. You need to start there with your thinking, because each social media channel is a platform with different functions and abilities. The nuance of digital involves a bunch of interrelated platforms and mediums for content. Each medium and content platform functions differently, and I'm going to break this down for clarity on utilizing each one well.

Mediums and Platforms

Mediums are the pieces of content, like written articles (on another site or your blog), images, gifs, videos, short text messages (could be in SMS, Tweet, Facebook), emails, and web content that is a page or combination of words plus image or video on a page of another site.

Platforms are the ways in which content and actions are presented. Platforms include everything from your site, Facebook,

Twitter, Tumblr, Petition sites, fundraising sites, Pinterest, Snapchat, SMS, and platforms to send email and host petitions connected to your site.

So here is the conundrum: Facebook, Tumblr, Snapchat, Instagram, Pinterest, YouTube, Google+, Reddit (kind of social), MySpace (still exists somehow) are all between fairly and very different social media platforms. And there are more with reasonable and niche followings. You would want a different content and engagement strategy for each. So how do you choose?

It's goal time. Is your goal to inspire action? Are you seeking to build a broader audience to engage around your issue? Do you want to use social media to build buzz for events? Recruit new people? Get more event attendees?

A good top-level place to start is thinking about how you are going to function as an organization, with the goals of the organization, and the resources you have.

Real Life Example -- Obama 2012 and Google+

During the 2012 election cycle, Google+ was just coming out. I thought it could be a game changer if it opened up a new platform of engagement. Joe Rospars and Teddy Goff, being the long seasoned Senior Digital Strategists that they are, cautioned any optimism until we could see audience and how it would really work. In 2008, a few people were constantly talking about Twitter, but couldn't answer how it could amount to votes. So as a platform, it didn't align with the campaign goals at the time. Then in 2012, it had matured as an online platform that was excellent at rapid response, building online conversation, and could be converted in actions like attending events. An intern at the time Danielle Butterfield- who now is quite a digital ads strategist - did some research and we made suggestions on how it could be used. It was piloted but ultimately the resources were pulled back, because even an organization that large had very finite resources and one goal. That goal was to get Barack Obama to 270 electoral votes, and anything that couldn't be benchmarked as adding to volunteers, dollars, or votes, wasn't worth the expense of money or human power. What are your 270 electoral votes? Is it winning an election, getting an initiative passed, protecting a river, defending human rights across the globe...? Whatever your goal is, you need to make critical decisions and answer if a platform is helping you meet that goal or drawing down resources.

Social Media, Catered to You

Here are a few real world examples on looking at different platforms based on size and scale. I'll give a few tips further on in how to think about different platforms in the Ecosystem of Content.

——You're Small and Abstract——

I spent some time six months ago talking to a partner foundation. They were getting pressure from the board to be better on social. We chatted for a bit so I could understand their goals. They didn't have an inherently large audience or a large base of donors. Funds came from large donors and not a large group of small donors, so their goal for social media was to offer a connection for those looking, and to alleviate the board's concern they weren't doing enough. Since their mission was to give grants and not spread messaging, I stayed focused on that advice.

I said you should do Facebook because it is expected. With the resources you have, I would just post grants and articles about grants. For sure, post some albums from events. It's enough to make the board satisfied, and enough content for those funders and people associated with the organization to find some content with which to connect. Since messaging isn't your mission, I don't think you'll ever have enough content to build much of a following in Twitter, so it's a bit of a take it or leave it. If you do it, try to post every other day or so. And I would recommend nothing for other platforms. By knowing goals, you can think about what the platforms are good at and if they're leverage-able for your project.

——You're Small and Local——

Different scenario - if you're working on a small local initiative or project, social media might be your best friend. Facebook can be very powerful for local organizing. If your goal is to connect with and organize people in a local community and their neighbors, it can go a long way. In most local campaigns, your goals would involve messaging, recruitment, events, and possibly turnout if it is an item to vote on.

Facebook could work great here using its Groups and Page features. Groups empower neighbors to engage and invite each other in, organizing local events together, thus allowing you to build action by making it clear that neighbors are supporting the campaign. Using a page and being small and local might make it hard to get the traction you need for Facebook to show your content in people's timelines. This is one reason groups are effective for local organizing because updates show up in your notifications. If you are going to set up a page, know that it might not get the consistent engagement you'd expect because of other pages and personal content muscling your page out of people's timelines. It might be worth exploring small boosts of even $25 targeted to locals you want to reach for engagement when needed.

There is an old saying in political campaigns that yard signs don't vote. This is true for major elections where all candidates have name recognition. But it isn't true when name or issue recognition are low. The signs can't vote, but it is valuable as a part of issue persuasion or education. Seeing someone you respect the opinion of get behind an issue validates it. This is very true online where we become peer-to-peer validators.

Would you use invest in Twitter? That's a good question. Do a number of your staffers or key volunteers really know Twitter and massaging? Would they have a strategy for finding locals to follow and engage with? Could you draft a strategy around that content leading to engagement? I do think it's okay in small campaigns and projects to let qualified volunteers help run online social. This isn't an endorsement of giving the keys to interns, but do you have someone that understands a platform well enough to engage in a strategy for the platform? If not, they probably shouldn't be driving it. The potential for harm is possibly greater than the return.

How do you know if you should use Instagram or Snapchat or YouTube? Again, it's about the goals. Are you trying to engage younger community members not using Facebook? (Although, it is a bit of a myth Facebook still has a reasonably high saturation rate among all age ranges). Do you know for sure they aren't there? If yes, do you have someone that understands how to use the platform? Not all platforms work well for engagement. If you are sharing messages from peer-to-peer, maybe Snapchat will work. If it's about protecting something beautiful or building something, the imagery of Instagram or Pinterest might have a use there. But the question should be: is going shallow in a few places better than deep on one of the bigger networks like Facebook and Twitter?

If you're a political campaign, yes to both Facebook and Twitter. You need to give people something to connect to and if you want to be in office you should be building a Twitter account to actually engage with constituents.

——— Moderately Sized Examples ———

So what if you are at a moderate to medium sized organization or campaign, maybe something with 10 to 20 people? At this point, you should have at least one, if not two to three people, involved in the digital realm. Social media is an element you should be considering in a real way, and you should put real consideration into how you want to maximize it. Let's split here a bit between electoral and NGO.

If you are an NGO, you're probably in this size, and you probably have either a service to deliver or an issue to make change on. How do you engage with people around your mission? That is a key question to finding your goal. The way you interact is fairly different if you are a service provider, an organization that needs people to drive messaging, or one that drives local issue organizing. Part of asking these questions is identifying your audience. If you are a service provider, your key audience should be figuring out how you can use social media to connect with those that might need your services and those that support your mission and want to help by volunteering or funding it. The question you should be able to answer long run is: are you engaging with those audiences?

This is a time to make a choice because you need to think about who is likely to be the core audience of your content. Is your audience who you serve, who you empower, or who you mobilize? Pick your main focus and develop content for them. It is okay to work content for different audiences, but with each piece you should know which audience you are intending to connect with. It is the social media equivalent of the right ask, right audience, right time.

Regardless of which way you go, I am going to suggest you be Facebook forward. It is still the largest, most robust social media platform. At this size, you should be planning on at least a piece of content daily. And think about how you could use it to connect new people to your organization. Will you drive the services you promote, possibly with a modest ad budget? Will you use events to ask supporters to invite in new people to your issue or cause? If you don't have skilled design folks on staff, I recommend hiring a graphic designer to make you a few templates you can update. Quality looking images go a long way in terms of reach and engagement.

Twitter is going to be a question of how you could and should use it. It can be a good place to find some people looking for services or volunteering. If recruitment like this is important, try the more advanced search features. At the very least, use it to drive updates about your organization. And having an account makes it possible for active users to link people to your organization. Planning should be about what the main focus is going to be. Is it engagement, messaging, or just updates? If it is to drive messaging or engagement, make sure you are investing enough time and energy so you impact the goals you want.

Other platforms are in the same boat as above. Does your mission lend itself to one of the niche platforms? Are you gaining in a strategic way by diverting resources here?

—— Electoral Moderately Sized Examples ——

In modern politics, you should have a social media strategy that is about messaging, connection, and engagement. These are three different, but interwoven, ways to use social media in an Ecosystem of Content.

You should have clear messaging filters through which your content is channeled. It should drive the words used and images selected. It should match up to your campaign's message and feel. If you're all business it should have that look and feel and consistent message. If you are all about the local community, your imagery and design should match up with that.

Because you are a political campaign, you should think about connection in a different way. What are the issues and characteristics you want to connect to the electorate with? You should be able to answer that, and plan content around it. Content created on a whim will only get you so far, and once in awhile, it might do very well, but possibly for the wrong reasons. Crafting good content builds a connection between the candidate and their constituents. It should be built around shared values and issues. Keep it real - people can spot fakeness on social media almost as much as in-person.

Take the message and connection you are building and translate it into engagement. Engagement on issues. Engagement on civic participation like registering to vote and getting others registered. And make sure to make asks to engage in the campaign. Ask people to get involved, tell them how they can do it, and respond when they show support or have questions. Have staff also positively engage supporters in comments and Twitter conversations.

Facebook should be a thoughtful mix of video messaging, issue content that is a mix of articles links and images, shareable images, and campaign events people can invite others to. At this level you should have a social media editorial calendar that you use to plan messaging and event building.

Twitter should also be a given. You should be using it to share campaigns messages. Show the candidate's personality and engage with supporters. I personally recommend also following folks in the community in which the candidate is running. There are pros and cons to this but I recommend a blanket strategy where you find very local accounts and try to proactively follow people you can identify, whatever the electoral district is.

You should have a YouTube channel at this level. You can drive people there and ask them to engage and share content. Keep an eye on what content is loaded with your campaign videos. Try to develop some content specifically to match up with what people might search about your campaign.

You should be thinking about the Ecosystem of Content. Can you design a suite of images on an issue that works well for Facebook and Twitter? Are you developing petitions or issue blogs on your website that work well for social sharing? Are you creating issue related petitions that recruit supporters from Twitter and Facebook to your email list?

Instagram, Snapchat, and other social media platforms are really going to be a balanced call again. You need to know what your in-depth strategy is. Is it worth going deeper to create more thoughtful content for other social media platforms? Whatever you do, don't hesitantly start a channel and stop. Would you want to elect someone who initiates a project and doesn't have a plan to finish it? Nope, you want to engage with an organization that has clear goals and a path to get there. Be that organization.

—— Organizational Scale NGO ——

What if you are at an organization or campaign, maybe with 20 to 50 people? I will stop here as well because I am roughly assuming once you fall into the 50 plus person size, you often have the budget to afford the consultants needed. This book as a goal is meant to serve folks that are in small to medium sized organizations to bolster support for their digital planning.

At a 20 to 50 person organization doing some kind of campaigning, I am hoping you have at least four to five people working on aspects of digital campaigning. In the staffing section too, we should be at a place where more staff are rolling digital into their role and thinking about how what they do translates to the internet.

Social media at this size should be very thoughtful. The Ecosystem of Content should be a thoughtful mix that drives your mission and works for each platform. Facebook is still an under tapped resource for most organizations. Do you have interplay between site content, Facebook posts, and email?

A way to think about this is to consider whether or not you're developing good content that is shareable and readable from Facebook. Are you tracking the engagement from the post back to the goal of the content? Is it an expanded reach of a conversion or conversion on a sign-up? Are you also developing content that will work well for sharing? Are you building your email channel from Facebook engagement? Do you then send emails to re-engage people with your page and to spread your organization's messaging, broadening the reach again and reactivating folks? You should be able to take your mission and benchmark engagement that drives your organization to that mission.

Facebook is not a novelty, but a way to drive and build engagement. You should have a serious plan on how communications and two-way engagement happen. If you want to follow good best practices with content types, the frequency of your posts should be at least three times a day, and not so close together that your content competes against itself. You will really start to see what resonates with your Facebook community. Now, don't only feed the community what it likes. Find the balance between the easy and shareable content with the deeper content you really want people to spend time with.

At this size you should certainly be thinking about some online ads budgets for Facebook content. I'm personally not a fan of buying page likes, because I think your content and an interplay with email should get you there. But I know firsthand when used well, it is an excellent platform for email list building and content engagement ads.

Twitter at this size is a must and you can take the elements above and really expand. I was asked a while back, what I would do differently if I were at a large political campaign again. The answer is, to have a role called "Architect of Story." Someone who structures how content rolls out from which voices online. Twitter is a perfect platform for this. If you are launching a new campaign, are there different points of view that different members of your organization would tackle it from? If so, could you think about how their voices play out and interact with each other on Twitter? Would one account tweet more about only the facts, another about the human connection, and another on how to take action? Could you have them retweet and interact with each other in an authentic way? Think about it as a place where people can interact with one another in a public and organized way.

—— Unscripted Twitter Reality ——

During the 2012 Obama campaign, I found myself in North Carolina meeting with an active Twitter user who I followed because I followed supporters in many states. They told me they appreciated the real interaction between the HQ staff, naming people they were following such as Mitch Stewart, Jeremy Bird, Yohannes Abraham, Betsy Hoover, and myself on Twitter. We would often tweet sports related jabs, retweet each other, and share snippets of in-person conversations. This volunteer appreciated that it humanized us beyond people they just got emails from. It made us real people beyond email sender names, and it deepened that supporter's engagement with the campaign.

So what would it look like if you intentionally invested in building out good content for staff accounts and encouraged a real cross handle engagement?

Tweets don't just go into the wind. They are the easiest piece of social content to track. I would encourage you to invest in a tracking system and look at what kind of message reach and conversion on goals you are getting. But please don't look at numbers for two months and say it doesn't work. Use benchmarks to figure out what does and doesn't work for you.

YouTube should also be used at this scale. I would encourage you to ask the question, what might someone search related to our campaign? Can we create a video that answers that search? How would we build a channel that is engaging, and maximizes the robust community on YouTube?

And we find ourselves at the question of whether or not to invest in Instagram, Snapchat, Pinterest, Tumblr, and other platforms. Again, this should be a real investigation into how it would impact your organization. At RAN, we had an Instagram account and built it as a secondary tier platform. Because we still had a lot more depth that we could achieve on Facebook and Twitter, it didn't make sense to invest in Instagram. The theory was simple: let's push simple content on Instagram that was previously created for Facebook. If it grows, that's great, but since we can't do link conversion from there, it would make more sense to invest in places where we could do conversion. If you have the luxury of a well-known organizational brand and you want to use Instagram to reinforce brand campaigns and engagement, I think that's a great goal. But make sure you've got a plan that establish benchmarks that make it clear what you're hoping to get from the channel.

—— Organizational Scale Statewide Electoral ——

This section is similar to what was discussed in the previous section for a moderately sized campaign. I would again raise real caution from going shallow into several platforms.

Instead I would think about what it looks like to have a very deep strategy in Facebook and Twitter. Be sure to use Facebook to really community build. Make it easy to connect to your campaign on Facebook and find ways to engage. Think about Facebook as essential to your messaging and community building strategies. Put yourself in the role of supporter and develop content that moves them through the Matrix of Engagement. Don't make it an afterthought; you want to be developing thoughtful Facebook first videos. Think through how this platform is essential in an Ecosystem of Content, moving people to your site, to email list, and back from those places to engage on Facebook. Often overlooked is the soft entrance of Facebook events. It can feel less daunting to sign-up for an event on Facebook with a new organization than a formal web form, but make sure you have a good strategy to go from your Facebook event to a database.

A good strategy should include running smart Facebook ads reaching for your target demographics for volunteering, registration, and turnout. Whatever it is, ads help you reach the core audience you are investing energy in reaching to begin with.

If you are planning to have an impact over these channels then you should be investing in training staff and volunteers on how to use Facebook and Twitter to reach campaign goals. What would such a plan look like for you? Ensure you have a good way to make it easy for supporters to share messaging and recruit others.

Here are a few deeper level considerations to get you thinking strategically:

Imagine you have someone from digital or communications take in a role like an "Architect of Story" mentioned in the NGO section above.

Think through how content could move and be promoted by all the staff in the organization.

Work on the possibility of you empowering organizers to be amplifiers.

Tell the story of the work such as sharing images of organizers connecting the community from their accounts, and amplified by communications staff and candidates.

Plan out organizers connecting with volunteers over social and working together to amplify core campaign messaging.

It is all about making sure your plan fits both the size of your organization and the goals you are trying to impact. Make conscious decisions about which platforms you are going to invest in with staff time and resources.

Platforms, The Ecosystem of Content, and The Matrix of Engagement

I want to be sure the underlying advice of planning doesn't get lost in any of the individual sections above.

You need to have a plan that takes into account that each social media platform is different. That plan also needs to be cognizant of a complete Ecosystem of Content.

An Ecosystem of Content is everything you use to engage users. Tweets, meta tags, subject lines, videos, URL names, and Facebook descriptions are all kinds of content. Social media is one of the most rapidly evolving spaces for real time, content-based engagement.

Content should be purposefully created for the goal you want to reach and the platform it's on. This means creating sign-ups and petitions that convert well from social media. URLs that are descriptive can be read on social before someone even clicks. Were you thoughtful about meta-images and content on the page for organic social media shares?

Is there interplay between Twitter, Facebook, email, site informational content, blog, and actions? Do you think about a new item going out across the ecosystem at large and which piece drives which?

Given that you have mission-driven goals, how are you thinking about a Matrix of Engagement and how does it play out on social? Think about ways to get to the right ask, to the right audience, at the right time. This isn't all about rapid response. It's about using social data, social recruiting, and driving message. Is the right ask to join a conversation on Twitter or push a new video on Facebook or YouTube? Is the right ask to make an email ask to use social for peer donations?

It's about time, planning, and action. If you are just getting started, don't let planning paralysis stop you. When I start working with a new group, we don't stop using social media until we have a plan. We look at where we are and discuss where we want to go.

Publish, Analyze and Publish

Don't be overly loose with social because major mistakes can set you back. The true beauty and curse of social media is volume. You have more space to experiment and test than most other spaces.

While Twitter and Facebook offer analytics in platform, I highly recommend getting a more sophisticated all-in-one publishing and reporting system. That way you can set up performance and benchmarking reports.

Running a thoughtful system in Google analytics and conversion goals is going to take you to that next level. Conversion tracking, set up and used correctly, allow you to see what content, sent when, on which platform, converts to what you want. It only works when used consistently and properly, over weeks and months. When the right data is collected over time, it tells you some really interesting information about where to dig in more and what opportunities are growing.

Good analytics used with thoughtful benchmarks are a perfect compliment to creative content. It tells you where and when the content is connecting with audiences. It will be an ongoing cycle of publish and analyze and taking that information to draft new content to publish again.

Site Content, Blogs, and Storytelling

They aren't just words for words sake. Site content, written copy, blogs, and storytelling should all link to your theory of change and advance your goals in an intentional way. So the question will always be: how does this drive you to your goals?

Let's explore how strong planning behind site content (images, words, videos, etc.) that appear on your website will lead to the impact you want. We'll also dig into how a blog can serve many functions and how you can strategically think about the ways a blog can highlight your organization, your work, your theory of change, and meet goals. We'll tie it all together with a bigger theory on storytelling. Storytelling should be the bigger lens through which most content flows because story, not facts and explanation, is what moves people. But storytelling also takes more time and resources. Storytelling doesn't just move people to action once; it helps build deeper and more long-term engagement from supporters.

Site Content

You only invest in content you have a clear plan for. Not just investing in paying outside support but in how you use current time resources. Well-planned content can lead to higher engagement around your issues, better conversions, and the impact you want. But you need to be intentional and be planning and iterating from creation to impact to promotion, and throughout review. That might sound like a lot, but simple tweaking should get you there. You can offer content in a very similar form to email. With email, we were focused on these three sections: Right Ask, Right Audience, Right Time. Site content is a bit more expansive, and has some of the same formal elements albeit a little different.

For each piece of site content, you need to think about Right Audience, Right Impact, Right Content and Layout. Now, content might feel a little redundant, but I'm using that in this case as a catch-all, since it may refer to words, images, videos, embeds from social, or another type of media form.

We have a content template available at www.TheDigitalPlan.com/ContentTemplate

Right Audience

Each section of the site should have an intended audience. This is who you intend to engage, convert, or sway. Now is the time to ask yourself, whom do you actually want to impact or empower with the piece of content? Not every possible bucket of people, you should just pick one. Consistently I watch people in the issue and political space write content without having one key audience in mind. Often, folks will list three to four different audiences, and it typically misses the mark for every possible audience.

It is okay to have a secondary audience. A secondary audience should always be the 'nice to have seen the content' or the 'nice to have engaged.' That means, not the primary target. You should know what your intended impact is to the secondary audience as well. If your primary target is a volunteer to engage with an issue, then maybe your secondary target might be a political or corporate institution you intend to move. While you aren't creating the content for the secondary target, what impact do you want them to feel if they see it?

Here are a few ways to think about right audience and why it matters. Often people confuse a secondary target for their primary audience. Possible audiences could be potential supporters and volunteers, current volunteers and supporters, potential large funders, media, a target you are attempting to sway, or someone who knows and cares about a certain issue. There are certainly more audiences and probably dozens of subsets of each so you should go as deep as you like or keep it as top line as possible.

Here is a list of simple questions to ask yourself for some of these key audiences:

Potential supporters and volunteers:

Does this content allow them to see themselves as a potential character in the content?
- This adds to relatability for the reader.

Is it clear how they can take action?
- This makes clear for reader how they can engage and for you it might be the goal you are trying to reach or a pathway to other engagement goals.

Is it clear what the problem and solution are?
- Problem without solution can feel overwhelming.

How do you make it clear that your action is a part of the solution?
- This raises the likelihood for engagement.

Is the content written in a way that is approachable and not overwhelming?
- Don't lose people by writing too narrowly or by being verbose.

Current volunteers and supporters:

How is this different from potential folks?
- Find ways to make it feel like it was written for people who are part of the tribe.

Are there phrases, organizational, or issue language that makes them feel like they are connected or on the inside of your project or issue?
- This helps bring that relatability even closer to the reader.

Have you shown how their work is part of the solution?
- So key in empowerment is showing the way for others.

Are there positive examples?
- These allow others to find what they want to model.

Did you intentionally choose to skip some introductory content?
- This will make it less applicable to new people but could make it feel more insidery.

Media:

Is there something unique and reportable in what you produced?
- Make sure that stands out from top to bottom.

Are there clear quotes and highlights?

- Use good layout choices to make that pop.

Is the access to quality imagery or video accessible for their reproduction?

- Consider having that linked at the bottom as to not slow down page load times.

Target you are attempting to sway:

Is your ask to them clear in the content?

- Similar to media make it clear from top to bottom.

Does the content make your organization's or communities' power clear?

- This is your narrative be sure to own it.

Does your content care more about simplicity or the complex nuance of the issue?

- This is truly your choice and has to do with whether or not your target will resonate more with big simple call outs or if the in-depth nuanced facts are important to them.

Someone who knows and cares about a certain issue:

Have you thought properly about the depth and engagement they might be looking for?

How did you make intentional choices between the balance of some introductory information vs. getting into the weeds?

Is there a way to make a simplified introductory version to make the content more accessible?

What do you know about the audience to design the content for them?

Two Stories on Audience

While at Organizing for America, the Democratic/Obama organizing committee that existed from 2009-2011, we built out a fairly consistent system of volunteer written content on volunteering. It was strongly advocating for Betsy Hoover, whose own belief in volunteerism and service was a core in the New Media (Digital) Organizing team. She helped lead a top-down belief in bottom-up organizing. From the beginning, we knew the target audience was current volunteers, with a secondary audience of potential volunteers. Why volunteer-produced content on volunteering written for other volunteers? That seems really meta.

First of all, it is an untold story outside of the final stretch of electoral campaigns. Yet, ongoing volunteering is critical to the health of the organization and mission. We had a well-known mantra of "Respect, Empower, Include." We knew that telling a story to this audience helped reforge these values we believed in because it was an organizing first organization and we believe featuring such stories truly respected the work on the ground. That it would also ensure that spotlighted volunteers would feel respected. Empowerment occurred in the drafting of content, and resonated in the words in the blogs. Inclusion appeared in the content itself. We were making a conscious choice to elevate the story of volunteerism and community organizing to front pages and social media feeds consistently.

While we didn't have the capacity to track the day-to-day impact of the lifetime volunteerism of individuals spotlighted, or to correlate volunteers who read it, the anecdotal data was still there. Volunteers who were spotlighted, often shared with staffers on many levels how appreciative they were of the opportunity to tell their stories. It made the volunteers who helped move the draft to publication feel more connected to each other and local staff. Feedback from volunteers who engaged with the localized volunteer stories, echoed similar appreciation even if they weren't the ones being spotlighted. Then other volunteers commented on how reading a piece of content made getting involved feel approachable. It became an important piece in the Ecosystem of Content that brought people into the organization and helped move them through what would be a full Matrix of Engagement.

* * * * *

Here is a different story about the right content presented to the right audience with shifting impact. Before I got to the Rainforest Action Network, the organization had worked on a major investment to connect the story of Conflict Palm Oil to the continued threat of the existence of orangutans. The audience was clear - they had narrowed down to moms in the U.S. as the main purchasers for children's snacks in the home. As they dug into their campaign against the Snack Food 20 - targeting 20 of the worst corporate consumers of raw palm oil - it was a key audience to impact the shift of their corporate targets.

They built out great collateral and launched a video about Strawberry the orangutan. The video was a success earning media and hundreds of thousands of views. Content was connecting with their target audience, and an organization that had a track record with more radical activists, was reaching what you would think of as typical everyday consumers of major snack brands. Folks signed online petitions and a few were willing to do some volunteering.

Then came higher level asks to take more action in their community. Join tactics like putting warning labels about conflict palm oil on products in stores. The action didn't happen. It was almost impossible to get the list of people they had recruited to take more radical action. At the end of the day, it was about the content the audience was designed for, being different from the new audience we needed.

In hindsight, it was easy to see that a second track of content designed for more radical activists willing to take more risks would have been ideal. That kind of content would have spotlighted that kind of action and encourage others to join. It was really about knowing what audience you need to engage or impact. To be clear, even though that original audience's engagement definitely shifted, a number of companies produced policies that lead to not purchasing Conflict Palm Oil, thereby protecting Indigenous communities, forests, and the endangered species living there. However, in the next phase when the companies were more dug in, a new audience and content created for that new audience was necessary.

Right Impact

By picking the right audience, you will be clearer on your intended impact. Sometimes it is getting a conversion on a fairly simple piece of site content like a donation page or petition. Other times, it is building engagement through readership of a blog or story or understanding the organizational theory of change. For each piece of content, you should be able to answer what the impact is. Not just impact, but how you will measure it. Measurement is key in knowing if you are lining up the work on the right content to the right audience to get the intended impact on your goals.

There are a number of ways to measure impact. Here are just a few.

Direct Measurable Impact

These are the impacts that are easy to measure like sign-up for an event. Sign a petition. Donate. Complete any number of discrete and trackable actions that you can assign a goal to.

External Measurable Impact

There are a number of ways to measure external impact. Earned media around the content is a validation by the press that your information or design of information has broader relevance. A way to measure it is how many stories or articles you are looking for post production. Another measurement could be getting partners to share and link to the content as validation. It means they value the contribution of the content to whatever the cause may be. Another might be how often the page is shared or referenced by supporters or others looking for information on your topic.

Measurable Next Steps

Sometimes the content we create doesn't have a specific ask. One way to measure in the digital space is to lead people deeper into your site. If a page has a high exit or bounce rate, you may want to consider revising or deleting it. If you can clearly see a connection from one piece of content to a next step or another information page, then that may be a worthwhile impact.

Anecdotal Response

Sometimes when we are pushing on a target like a company, politician, or institution, we have to look at movement from them as a goal. If you are trying to move one of these targets, is there a way to infer if it hit the mark? You might know you moved them if, after launching, someone from the target group confirmed a meeting to discuss next steps, or if they released a statement on the issue you are pushing. It could even be your messaging or a rebuttal appearing in their communications.

An internal anecdotal response could be hearing from supporters about how it changes their feeling or connection to the organization, campaign, or issue.

Increased Engagement

If you have the luxury of a system that captures data well, you can seek correlations between certain pieces or types of content you produce with other actions like donations or volunteering.

If you don't have that luxury, look for patterns where content (and content referenced) connects to, supports, and leads them to further engagement.

Raw Views

At the very least, set a number of page views you might want for the content. If you believe the content is clearly moving the needle on your impact, then decide what number of page views would look like a success. Set a value for the number of views you need to move forward in a meaningful way. Would having 100 or 1,000 views that engage supporters over a month be worth the content being produced? To get to an answer there, you might need to dig into a bit of your own site's historical analytics. Make sure it is about moving your clear campaign goals and how these views get you closer.

Right Content and Layout

Now that you have the right audience and right impact, you just need to connect to the right content. This is where Right Audience + Right Impact + Right Content and Layout = Change. It really is all about the combination of content and layout. Make sure you've thought through things like supporting imagery and video.

To choose the right content, pick the one main message this piece needs to convey. Back to goals - what is the goal of this piece? How will you deliver it to the audience? Keep thinking about the goals while going through production. More often than not, you can simplify and let good content be good content.

Once you have clearly written down main message, audience and impact, make sure you clearly understand your container. This is why content and layout are twin pillars. Are you drafting petition information that is normally less than 300 words or are you drafting a long form story? Make sure you understand how you are going to introduce and close the content.

Think through the layout of all content, I really mean it, apply this to all site content. Too often, folks don't apply this thinking to simple pages like donate pages. My experience time and time again is when you apply good content theory to all content, you increase engagement. Does the donate page language match whatever content may have taken the user there? Is it still clear why this action matters? Is it simple enough to skim and take the action? If not, there must be a really compelling reason to lower conversions. Maybe you have a special fund and you need to make very clear to supporters exactly where the money is going. It might be worth dropping your conversion rate by a few percentage points if the long run experience is better.

While I can't offer a silver bullet on how to layout your content, I can offer a few simple tips to help you make decisions. Look at others doing what you want to do. Especially look at well-funded larger entities. You want to know who spends a lot of time worrying about users reading to the end of an article? Media companies. You want to know who spends a lot of time page conversions and donations? Look at the bigger organizations in your field. Learn, model, and test what works for you.

Blogs

There are so many great things you can do with a thoughtful blog. Many organizations rarely answer the questions: Why do you have to have a blog? Why? What purpose does it serve your organization? Even if your organization has had a blog and you are thinking about revamping it, then you should what the goal of your blog is. Here are a few ways to approach blogs:

- The Catch-All blog, this is what most organizations use and, while I won't fault you for it because of capacity, the reality is they are rarely engaging.
- Storytelling blog, now this is where organizations connect with people.
- Issue/Department/Function Themed Blog, when done well is an expansion of storytelling to cover broader issues and topics.

Thinking through any of the following approaches and uses could be fine depending on your organization, but you should know what you intend to do with it. Otherwise consider opting out of it. That's okay too. But remember when done well, blogs are an important piece in an ecosystem of content and engagement.

The Catch-All Blog

Most organizations just put up random information and they don't intend to post as stand alone pages to their blog. It works if that's your only goal. If you are hoping to inspire readership don't expect it to catch one. No one wants to wade through your press releases, stories, organizational funding updates, and programmatic changes in the same stream. Would you read that? I wouldn't. The individual pieces might get life if you share them via email or social media, but you aren't likely to see return readership. That's okay as long as you know this is your goal and expectation.

Storytelling Blog

These are rare. But some organizations do find a way to write a compelling ongoing narrative about the organization. When done well, they will certainly raise organizational engagement and affinity. You will need to have a really functional content production calendar and system for remaining consistent. It takes an investment in time (and possible staff) that is inherently money to organizations.

Issue/Department/Function Themed Blog

Most blogs I see look a little more like this. It is a hard model to either break away from or make great. Organizations often do many things and they want to tell the story of them all. You might use tags and categories to try and make the content feel connected.

I have yet to see the connection link into a coherent narrative. Most likely you'll be relying on the one off pieces of content being driven by other engagement channels. Here you should still be thinking about how you close individual blog posts to get the impact you want. A link to another article or action or donation for instance.

While at RAN, we began a long journey into restructuring our content into ways that allowed people to read a piece of content and see how it fit into broader issues and campaigns. NGO and political campaigns are so often geared to just the linear timeline and workflow that it makes shifting how we produce and manage content difficult. So how do you create content that is a narrative people can drop into and go deeper if they want to? Although campaigns internally function in a linear way, everyday there will (or should) be new people making a connection to the issue or organization. How do you get them up to speed and engaged in a meaningful way? Certainly a mishmash of not concretely related content linked via tags is not the way. I truly believe organizations that tackle those questions will unlock greater engagement than they ever have before. Have a long view of goals and campaigns, and structure your blogs in a way that make it easy to connect to information over time. This allows users to drop in and connect to an issue in a fluid way. This will inherently expand your engagement and move the needles greatly toward your goals.

Storytelling

Gathered around the campfire, the radio, the TV, the laptop, and mobile device, humans find themselves most drawn to story. Storytelling is a cross-cultural human experience so why do organizations keep trying to move people with facts and process? More often than not, the individuals in organizations who manage policy and campaigns feel deeply connected to an issue. They themselves are deeply swayed by facts. It is true; there is a subset of the human population more swayed by facts than story. But the reality is, this subset is smaller than the audience you most likely need to make change.

Great digital work empowers storytelling across platforms, expands audiences, and creates greater impact. It is a thing you can strategically plan for.

The following sections are a few ways to embrace storytelling.

Human Scale of a Major Issue

All too often, issues feel beyond our impact. Take climate change or gun violence, for example. When stated by name, these issues feel wildly beyond one's ability to change anything. If you stay in the big statistics and facts, it is overwhelming. To move people, hone in on one specific story, (yes, in a single piece of content) and try to keep it to one. Don't go light touch on several stories crammed into one piece of content. Pick one that illustrates the problem. It is okay to weave in the bigger statistics but you need to express them in a way that the reader can relate on a human level.

For climate change, for example, can you connect people to someone immediately impacted? Don't hang in the space of the entire community. Use the community to get even closer. Find a way to describe what these immediate impacts mean, such as how unstable life is, how it feels, and how those feelings ripple into every aspect of life. Then present the possibility of change in a realistic manner. Link that human level story to what's next for the person in the story so that the reader can find connection.

Reader as Ally

You can create a narrative about impact humans, the ones making change on issues, where the reader can clearly draw a line as an ally. Can you show impact from others like the reader? Find a way to make it clear that there is a way to be supportive. Don't leave folks in the gloom of the story, but make it clear there is a way to be supportive with time or funding.

Reader as Change Agent

Reader as a change agent works best when you can model the behaviors of another. Like the story of about Obama volunteers above. It was a place where the narrative wasn't about Obama or leaders in Washington D.C. but everyday people working for change. Find that story you can tell that allows some to vividly see what it would look like for them to be a change agent.

Tell a story that includes common barriers. Barriers could be time, money, and systemic pressure. Find a way to walk the reader through the way in which someone else overcame such barriers. In these stories, don't reach for the super-heroic; that's a hard place for others to see themselves. Go for the everyday common person and leave the super-heroic for the ally stories where someone wants to support the heroine or hero. Find those everyday traits and emphasize those.

Heroes and Villains

A tried and true storytelling device is creating two clear sides and one clear villain. In this story format, you make clear the heroic traits of the individual, team, or organization you want readers to align with. You then cast the opposition as a villain where reviled traits are clear.

I have to be honest - Heroes and Villains isn't my favorite storytelling approach. Not because it doesn't work, but because I think so much of what is a mess in the current state of American politics is over simplified use of this storytelling device. There is an inherent polarization that happens with this kind of story.

If you want to draw a distinct line, this is a very powerful device hence its rapid use in media narrative. You should also know that when used, it is hard to walk back from painting someone as a villain. But if long-run relationships aren't important, think about how you can pull on traits of hero and villain. Tug them and make it clear your reader can be part of the heroic team. This could be used by framing them as an ally to the heroes or by showing them how they themselves are an agent of the rebel alliance.

Summary

Take time and be intentional about site content and the layout you choose so you can achieve the impact you want. Blogs can serve many functions and you can strategically think about the ways a blog can highlight your organization, your work, your theory of change, and meet your goals. It is up to you to be strategic about your approach. You can tie it all together with storytelling and narrative. Being thorough in thinking about the Right Audience, Right Impact, Right Content and Layout will mean finding a path through storytelling. That path will help you achieve your goals.

Digital Ads

This section only applies if you have budget for digital ads, but it may also be the section that helps you make the better case for digital ads.

Let's start with the case for digital ads and how they can impact your goals. Specifically, the power digital ads have to connect to new audiences, reconnect with existing audiences and deepen further connections. Then we'll breakdown ways to think about ad use when it comes to conversions, impressions, and views. Each outcome is a different goal - the most common outcomes or goals are conversions, impressions, and views. You should frame your strategic plan for digital ads around these goals. We'll pull that together with tips on planning digital ads to make the impact you want.

The Case for Digital Ads

Digital ads can help you reach the right audience at the right time. The buzz around digital ads is well deserved, even if somewhat misunderstood. Digital ads aren't a replacement for other good strategies but should be viewed as good argumentation to your other plans. Let's breakdown how you use digital ads to connect to new audiences, to reconnect or deepen connections, and to influence the influencers.

Reaching New Audiences

Used well, digital ads can allow you to connect to new audiences with precision and focus. First, you need to know whom the audience is that you want to reach. If you can identify your target audience, it will be easier to gauge if your ads are performing well. Let's give a concrete example.

Say a number of ads vendors want to focus on a surface level deliverable like CPA (cost per acquisition) of a new email address to your list. If someone says industry standard is $1.50 to $2.00, that sounds like a reasonable metric. And using a number like CPA as a top line metric - the main metric by which you are measuring success - often makes sense, but how do you know if these emails will be valuable to you?

The questions you need to be able to answer are: what is it you hope cohorts of emails will do immediately or over time? Is your goal to build a list of potential donors? Potential online action takers? Something else? Knowing a goal of what you want the new audience to do will let you know if you are on track. If long-term donation is important to you, then you should be tracking immediate donation (some call it immediate upsell) or long-term donation history of sent emails. An immediate donation from a cohort of ads running is a good indicator if that group is likely to donate in the long run.

Similarly, if you have a particular call to action that is very specific to an issue, you are more likely to get repeat action from those emails. But you might not get broader organizational connection unless you find ways to connect them through other content using a solid Matrix of Engagement theory.

New audiences can also be people connected with your content including videos, blog posts, and social media graphics. If you are in an awareness-raising phase, ask yourself whom you need to reach. Without knowing whom it is you need to reach, it is too easy to mis-manage a budget for such ads. The power of digital ads allow you to do amazing targeting based on a full range of demographics and interests to see if the ads make the connection you want.

Like no medium before, digital ads let you see results in real time, test, test, and refine your message. Used well, you can test message and refine based on the actual engagement you get. I do think there are still many reasons to create print mediums (like bumper stickers and signs) and traditional media (like billboards, TV, and radio) because they still have an impact on certain niche audiences. Digital ads empower you to see results with hard statistics and connections, both immediately and with better tracking over time.

Reconnecting

Digital Ads don't just let you connect to new audiences, they also allow you to connect to audiences you have already met. As you probably experience yourself, there are causes you care about but you miss their content in your Facebook timeline or don't open every email they send. Platforms like Facebook allow you to serve ads back to people who already like you or have stopped responding to emails.

Think about what content might get someone back and feeling connected to your cause, and which audience you want to reach with the content. Do you have a cohort of long time email subscribers that you have some data on about their interests? Is there active content in the form of a sign up or petition that might get them reactivated? Someone you already have a connection to is likely to be very low hanging fruit.

Deepening Connection

The more you can build affinity between your issue or campaign to a person, the more long-term engagement that is likely to occur. There are so many ways to think about audience but here are a few to get your ideas flowing.

Your audience is already active, and you want to take it to the next level. Is there a particular cohort of people you have that are active and you want to make another ask of them? Maybe you are worried too many asks may cause them to unsubscribe from your email list. We've all been there - the last group you want to lose is your most active. A tactic that could work for you is to serve them the ask via a promoted social media post.

Perhaps you are starting a new campaign or talking about a new issue and want to orientate an active audience to it. If it is important to you to foster a good relationship with a group you've invested in forming, consider sharing content with them and track whether or not it reaches them via paid ads.

Maybe you have folks on your list or following you on social media that aren't particularly active. You can think about testing different rounds of social media content with them to raise connection. It could be sign ups and petitions if you want to get them to make a firm commitment to an issue or type of engagement. Or it could be content in the form of a blog post or video if you think greater issue connection or knowledge is what is added to move them.

Goals for Tracking Impact

We now have some broad framework to think of audiences including appealing to new audiences, reconnecting with an old cohort and deepening engagement with an existing group.

Now let's talk about how to think about goals to make sure your ads have the impact you intended.

Conversion Goals

Conversion goals are often the easiest to quantify and validate ad spending. These are goals that lead to a direct online action. That action could be a donation, signing a form, or some sort of online petition. These kinds of goals work great when you know exactly the kind of online conversion you are looking for.

The next question to ask is, what is it worth? This can be a lot less straightforward and takes some internal thinking. What are you - as an organization - willing to pay for a petition signature of someone entirely new to the list? Is there an active petition that you need to reach a target goal on in order to pressure a target? In this case, what is it worth to get current list subscribers to sign on? Is it more valuable for early names to show momentum or later names to get across the finish line or both?

Sometimes people confuse new email sign-ups to their lists for their target audience and don't factor in the cost for the list they really want. While it might make sense to get a decently targeted general list, if you want people to take a very specific action, you should figure out what that's worth to you.

Case Study -- Expensive Sounding Sign-Ups

During the Obama 2012 campaign, we were exhausting our list for new recruits to our fellowship program. I had been working with our training team, led by Sara El-Amine, on how to optimize the sign-up forms and plans for recruiting. Working with the web development and analytics team we were able to find the right volume of questions per page and the multi-step experience to increase people completing a fairly long application online.

Complete applications made it easier for staff on the ground to prioritize applicants who were serious. The barriers to entry, while very high by online standards, meant the staff with already limited capacity could work with a pool of applicants more committed to joining. Yet the barriers were not too high to dissuade people who were interested. After several successful rounds of emails and social media promotions, we realized most states were off of their goal of recruited fellows.

I approached the internal ads team to figure out an ads strategy. They were reluctant because the cost was likely to be prohibitive. We ran a pilot in one state and the results (with some optimization in language) was still coming in at about $10 per completed form. After the state worked through applicant outreach, they confirmed 1 in 10 to the program, meaning they had a $100 cost per qualified lead. Sounds expensive right?

It was actually an entirely reasonable rate. These ads allowed the team to hit their goals of fellows recruited. Those fellows in turn were going to learn about community organizing and would be directly responsible for authentic voter engagement in their community. Empowering new organizers and reaching targeted voters crucial to the election was easily worth $100 per fellow. But we could have never answered that authentically without knowing how to look at the cost and value of our goals.

Impression Goals

A slightly softer goal type is the impression goal. We all know branding works. There are even political campaign strategies to index how many pieces of content a voter needs to see before being swayed. With some variation from studies, some report seven touches via mail, phone, in-person or otherwise is all it takes. We know there is some sway from billboard effects on people, and studies on that really vary.

Think of impressions as online billboards. If your content is clear and concise, an impression can be part of a larger engagement strategy. To measure, you need to be willing to let a campaign run and see if you can test with a cohort for a shift in behavior.

An example would be an ad you allow to run repeatedly to an audience in hopes of an impact at a later date. Not just hitting the audience once, but allowing for repeat impressions to lead to later action around a targeted issue.

View Goals

Sometimes the goal is to spread a message. Raw view goals may be exactly what you are looking for. It's important to note that different ad platforms count views in different ways. Make sure you are reporting on what you really want to be. This number will change over time, so confirm how many seconds into content a platform counts as a "view" for accurate data.

If you think education on an issue is key, view goals are great metrics for that. Think about what the audience you think is most important to view the content, and what the value of each view would be for you.

A tip about online video and especially paid views - the place where people drop-off from a video can be pretty telling about the content. Does the drop-off happen at a particular transition? Do they drop where the video switches from storytelling to heavy facts? Use this data to inform your content and how you want to develop it going forward, or consider editing and rerunning the ads.

Digital Ad Planning and Budgeting Tips

Here are a few tips to help you get the most out of your ad planning and maximize the impact of your budget.

ABT - Always Be Testing. You should always have variation in copy and imagery for ads you run. Test and see what performs best. This also goes for email subject line testing. Test the ads with part of the audience and then expand the audience on the one performing better.

Ads as a Social Messaging Test. Most social media ads platforms offer what is often called "dark posts." These are posts that don't show up in follower timelines and are only seen by those served ads or those who shared the imagery. This can be a great way to test messaging and see which resonates better with your audiences.

Keyword search on search engines is a prime opportunity for low hanging fruit. Someone already searching for your issue or organization is one click away from some sort of action. Make sure you are matching those searches to the action you want to engage them with.

Make the budget around your goal, not your goal around your budget. I recently heard an organization ask how voters can be registered with $2,000. Yes, they will get some sort of answer and many ad firms would just go ahead and help them spend that money. The questions should start with how many voters you want to register and how you build a budget from there.

Summary

We talked about how digital ads can impact your goals in very tangible ways. Digital ads can help you to connect to new audiences, reconnect with existing audiences and deepen connections. You now have some distinct ways to think about ad use and goals when it comes to conversions, impressions, and views. Developing goals that are thoughtful about audience, outcome, and budget will help create a digital plan that has a positive impact.

Data and Analytics

I always say good digital is a mix of creative art and hard science. Data and analytics are the hard science part. The science side allows you to monitor and see how your creative work is interacting and engaging with people.

Let's walk through a number of important pieces of data analytics to have a solid grasp of some best practices to make your digital planning solid. Knowing site analytics and some basic ways to make good decisions with that data is crucial. We'll dive into email analytics, using data well, and building out a smart data library. Then we will talk about social media analytics and the difference between vanity metrics and deeper engagement metrics. We'll wrap up with some tips to help you make the most of your Data and Analytics.

Site Analytics

Websites are still the backbone of most organizations and campaigns wishing to maintain relationships with supporters online. Yes, you may engage and community build on social media platforms. But the place where you can deeply build supporter data and knowledge depth, is on your website.

Site analytics help you learn a lot of things about supporters. I highly recommend setting up Google Analytics. It's free, well documented, and very extensive. We'll approach this section from the framework of Google Analytics. Feel free to use whatever platform you prefer, but we will be discussing Google Analytics because of its accessibility.

Page Engagement

Understanding site traffic helps you make better plans for where to prioritize your efforts and how to change your plan for engaging with people. It's important to understand your overall site traffic and what pages people currently engage with. Look at what pages are getting the most traffic. Does it line up with the pages you planned to promote via email, social, media and ads? If not, where are people coming from?

Is the amount of traffic you are getting on pages worth the investment in time on that page? A good way to think about this is if you are getting 20 to 30 page views a month on a page, is it worth prioritizing an overhaul? The answer might be yes if that's a page major donors often use. But the answer might be no if it was the download page for a flyer you thought hundreds of people would use.

It is also important to know about exit and bounce rates because a lot of traffic to a page can look good, but if the bounce or exit rates are high, that means people either didn't find what they were looking for or you didn't provide them with a next step. Bounce rate means they entered the site on that page and then just left. Exit rate means they were on at least one (if not more) pages before they decided to leave your site.

More often than not, sites have the most traffic on the pages with content you promote most on social media, email, and digital ads. You should dig in and see if your traffic lines up with that. Are there some outlying pages that are performing exceptionally well? What can you learn from those pages? There are many ways to interpret exit and bounce rates and being aware of these rates will help you to make more informed decisions.

Decisions Based on Analytics

While at Rainforest Action Network, we went through rebuilds of the website to solve for a variety of problems. In the second rebuild, we made conscious decisions to include as many things as possible on the homepage. This certainly flies in the face of prevailing winds of minimalism, but what we were trying to solve for was actually internal friction.

Knowing that most site traffic to date was flowing in from digital ads, email, and social media, I didn't have a high priority for overly focusing on the homepage. I wanted it to be thoughtfully orienting to new visitors, but did not want to spend as much time refining it as much as we would for the high traffic page types. But the digital team was likely to spend disproportionate amounts of time fielding requests to include things on the homepage. To avoid that, we planned to load up the homepage with everything someone might be looking for. There were some bugs in how some of the content was featured, but that's not why we chose to recreate the homepage.

After three months of consistent data checking, we were actually getting a lot of site traffic through the homepage. It seemed to have a strong correlation to the new user traffic from ads and our increased work with SEO and Google AdWords. Looking more closely at the traffic however, it was a scattershot of pages people went to next, and we weren't getting them onto pages with priority information.

We took that data and endeavored to recreate a better homepage that included more orientation to the organizational content. We were more thoughtful on the amount of ease people would have to find the latest (and organizationally deemed most important) information. Had we not used data to make the decision, we may have just cleaned up the page and kept the "everything on the homepage strategy" but we couldn't ignore the amount of valuable traffic we were losing to the scattershot of next pages. We instead were able to make a well-informed series of decisions about what to feature for people to transition them to valuable engagement to move our goals forward.

Conversions and Sourcing

One of the features I love about Google Analytics is setting up conversion goals. Essentially, you are setting up systems to see how many people who visit a page take a targeted action. You can set it up for a wide range of activities like signing a form or petition, making a donation, and downloading or engaging with a piece of content. Conversion goals empower you to know if the audience you are getting to the page took the actions you wanted to get there. If you have a reasonable email list size and petitions are important to you, and you increase conversion percentage by just a few percentage points, you may be adding thousands of engagements. Similarly, if you actively send a lot of fundraising asks, generating a better conversion rate in donations could lead to thousands of dollars a year.

A wonderful way to even more deeply understand conversions and engagement on a page is to set up sourcing. Sourcing allows you to know how traffic arrived to your site, down to the exact page it comes from. You can set it to be pretty granular with the data down to an individual piece of social media content level and it can help you identify which piece of content brought in the traffic and engagement on the site. I would encourage you to dig in online or ask a sourcing specialist to help you come up with a system that works for you.

Sourcing for Growth Planning

While supporting the Nevada state staff for Obama 2012, we were working heavily on event building and there were going to be heavy rounds of surrogates in the state. I was sent in to help triage the state's digital program for the last 10 weeks of the campaign.

The state's social media numbers were pretty small - one of the many reasons I was sent in. But when I looked at the sourcing for how people were signing up for events in Nevada, it was clear to me that a large portion was from social media. That set in motion a plan to bolster social media growth with a focus on using it for event turnout. We were able to make gains in growth and the overall percentage of event attendees sourced to social media went up in correlation.

Email Analytics and Your Database

Core to so many organizations, projects, and campaigns functioning well, is a healthy email program. That's covered in that section called email. To make the most of your email program, you need to be aware of analytics and testing. There are the basic email tests like the subject line test, which is ideally used for every email send. In every subject line test, you should look at open rate, click rate, action, unsubscribe, and spam.

Open rate is a good barometer of whether or not a small piece of content contains a subject line that connects with people. If your open rates are lower than you expected, it could be worth considering another test or two.

Click rate and **action rate** are prime indicators of whether or not the content in the email tracked with the subject line. It also shows if the email content was compelling enough for your audience to engage in the ask. **Unsubscribe rates** are another way to understand if your content was what people expected when they signed up.

Testing can, and ideally should, take broader looks beyond individual email analytics. You can see over time how cohorts of people behave based on their past engagement with you. Think about tests to see if certain sender names have different connections for people over time. One of the most important things about testing is understanding how your data changes over time because it will help you identify useful trends related to your website and audience. If you wanted to know if people on your list truly prefer email on Sunday or Wednesday, you will need to run that study over time. You should find ways to control for similar pieces of content.

I've seen a number of people "test" fairly significant things just once or twice - such as day or time of an email send - and make bold predictions from it. Yes, that is technically a test, but it isn't a very valid test. I also recommend testing again over time. What holds true today may be different in 6-12 months. If you use smart, well-designed tests, you'll be able to make smart informative plans.

To do this kind of testing, you'll need a good database, and you'll need to put information in there. It's important to ask yourself what kind of information you would like to know about your supporters to create better email preferences. If you don't have the answers today, can you start building out that data? Are there certain elements of data that your database inherently captures? For the data it doesn't capture, you will want to create a system of tags that you can assign to people based on interest and behavior. If your database doesn't allow for that, seriously consider migrating.

Unless you have a person just focused on data, I highly recommend minimizing the number of databases you use. Every migration back and forth is likely to cause errors. A number of times over the years, even on high functioning teams, I've seen data imports forgotten or messed up. Each import is a chance for error and probably an operational cost you haven't budgeted time for so take some time to do the research, consider your goals and choose wisely.

Data Library

Like all good libraries, a data library helps you stop and make sense of things. Far too many times, I've seen organizations start making tags for different information in their database and rely on institutional memory to know what each meant. Even the ones created by current staff members often forget the nuance of the tag originally created. I highly recommend creating an online spreadsheet that everyone shares.

In the spreadsheet, make very clear what each tag means. Creating a tag hierarchy and similar structures for similar actions and events will also help you to maintain consistent data that is easy to interpret.

Master Issues vs. Sub Campaigns

Let's say you work on Water Issues, Poverty Issues and a few that overlap. For the water-focused campaigns, you might assign something like Water_Access to people who signed up for things related to water access and Water_Clean_Flint for people concerned about the campaign for clean drinking water in Flint.

If you were hosting events, you might consider adding codes to abbreviate types of events so you could see who attended or signed up for a particular event. It might be an additional tag and you would add that to your library like PB for phonebook or PC for press conference. That might look like Water_Clean_Flint_PB or PB_Flint depending on the structures that make the most sense for you.

A good data library over time will help you know your audiences better and make more accurate decisions when drafting plans.

Social Media Analytics

Data varies wildly based on the social media platform being used. For example, Facebook is a more sophisticated, very data rich platform whereas Instagram is very limited. The important thing to figure out is what metrics matter to you and why. There are a number of articles on vanity metrics that include social media likes and basic reach, and while I agree with them on some levels, I think they undervalue some key pieces of engagement.

The number of Likes and Followers you have matters. Those things are a measure of potential reach and social validation. It's also hard (nearly impossible) to have meaningful numbers of conversions on a petition with only 100 Facebook likes. So if you are just getting started, ignore the folks that say all that matters is conversions from the content. You probably don't have that kind of capacity. Good content - meaning content people engage with via shares, likes and retweets - is the only thing that will bring you conversions later.

If you have capacity, then by all means, dig in and do research on which content is resonating with people. If you figure out sourcing, you can actually look at which tweet and Facebook posts actually drive sign-ups on petitions or attendance for events.

Data and Analytics planning is all about which numbers are going to move your big goals. Take some time and understand them. Good data should enable you to better prioritize and plan around what happens on your site, across email and social media platforms so they all consistently tell a story about your work.

Learning frameworks for analyzing your data is easier now more than ever. Take a moment and dig into the plethora of free courses out there on analytics. Understand what is behind your numbers and be authentic about when you do and don't know what they say. I've watched a number of people misinterpret what a particular social media's post reach meant about a social media program at large. They didn't take the time to understand the mechanics of the platform and what kind of bigger trends were at play in the content. Had they had a stronger grasp of analytics and applied that lens, they would have seen a different and more accurate picture. This is similar for site content as well. If you are getting very few views, it is up to you to know if that is roughly the expected and maybe still valuable number, or if new strategy is needed.

Summary

Now you have a basic framework for ways to think about site traffic and using those numbers to make decisions. From those basics, you can dig into sourcing content and tracking conversions on your site so you can answer more finely grained questions. You should now be able to talk about important top line metrics for email like open rate, click rate, action, unsubscribe, and spam rates. We went deeper to make sure you understand good tagging and what quality testing could dig more deeply into. A good database is key to making any of that work and a data library is key to making sense of the information you are collecting. Cultivate deeper insights into social media analytics and know what sort of numbers to focus on depending on the stage of your project or campaign and the reality of resources. If you bring all of these different data outlooks together and use them to inform your work, you will inherently create stronger digital plans.

Digital Organizing

Digital Organizing is my passion because good digital organizing is about understanding all of the facets that make up the sphere of digital strategy. Implementing thoughtful strategy can be used to engage, empower, and impact your goals.

I've seen the term digital organizing thrown around in very loose terms, especially in regards to what it means for staff and what they do. So we'll start this chapter on how to frame and think of digital organizing as a concept and a role. From there we'll dig into ways to think about supporter-based digital organizing, then we'll expand out to partner organizing. This chapter will close with some final thoughts on organizing principles to make the impact the world needs you to make.

What is Digital Organizing?

I think of Digital Organizing as the online manifestation of community organizing. Community organizing as defined by Google is, "the coordination of cooperative efforts and campaigning carried out by local residents to promote the interests of their community." Digital Organizing is about using the internet to either bring together a community or leverage the internet for a community already working together.

I've heard of a few people reference the role of Digital Organizer by describing tasks rather than vision for the role. Sometimes it is a set of tasks that support traditional field organizing, like supporting event creation and data. I would caution calling that role digital organizing and would liken it more to Organizing Support. Someone in that role may not be endeavoring to actually organize themselves. Other times I've heard the role referenced to someone who is sending emails. Well that too sounds more like an email campaigner. Understanding how to apply the term "Digital Organizer" appropriately will help you to clarify your goals for your digital plan.

A Digital Organizer should be either building community or helping others leverage online tools to win campaigns. Online community can occur in a number of ways including forums, email lists, and listservs, and even around social media channels. What makes digital organizing specifically descriptive is that it is less about the *tasks of digital tools* and more about the *how*. The *how* of digital organizing is often about relationships between a cause and its supporters. Strategically cultivating online communities should involve intentionally building relationships and utilizing community power to work together in a coordinated way for a coordinated cause. That is the role of a Digital Organizer.

Digital Organizing for Causes and Community

Online community can take many forms. As mentioned above, it can form in forums, email lists and listservs, around social media channels, or in intentionally created community building spaces and groups online.

Healthy online communities have norms which make the purpose of the group clear, describe how to get invited and (to some degree) who is welcome. Good organizing doesn't mean everyone has to be invited, which also means it is okay to ask or help the trolls to leave. Just like in-person community dynamics, we make clear what commitments are, and the expectations for how members of the group should conduct themselves.

Sometimes community is entirely organic and self-organizing. But if you are reading this book, you have goals and things you want to impact in the world. Good digital organizing can help you meet those goals as long as you are intentional about what you want and how you are going to get there.

Community in Forums

My first paid online work was for a company that developed fantastic Miami-based travel, tourism, and local information called, MiamiBeach411.com. I was first drawn to the forums as I was relocating to Miami, and I appreciated the real dialogue about life and support in Miami. The website also created great localized information and content, which is where my first online writing appeared. There was a true community based vision created by the founder Gus Moore.

The site itself is still an amazing model for developing and moderating great local information and online community. We see such behavior across the internet and often take it for granted, such as group sourced tech support on pages like Apple.com and Amazon.com. The reason online interaction works well in all of these places because of clearly set rules of conduct on how to engage, and clarity on who is a moderator with definitions on how things are moderated.

The early years of the Obama campaign were also host to online forums that allowed for great organizing. Now, I understand that forums can be troubling and difficult but you also don't have to build your own. Do you have an authentic connection to Reddit Forums or other places on the internet? There is a lot of benefit for helping a self-moderated forum grow into the activists and ambassadors for your cause.

Intentionally Built Community

The Call Tool. During the 2012 campaign a great example of Digital Organizing you probably haven't heard much about is the Call Tool team. Sometimes naming simplicity is best. It was managed by Bridget Halligan who managed both the tech production of the call tool and building an online community to engage around the tool.

The tool itself would be deployable by state staff as a remote calling device for local volunteers and as the centerpiece of a national Call Tool team. But from experience, the campaign knew that building an all-online community could lead to big results that impacted voter engagement goals. The manager went to great lengths to connect with volunteers who would become leaders. She invested time in building community and team identity. Most importantly she made the goals of the teams clear and held people accountable.

Digital Organizing isn't just about building community. It should be about impact and reaching goals. This program had its ups and downs from data to function issues like all programs do. Even its share of community issues. But staying focused meant reaching more voters than would have been reached with just local state work or by just emailing alone.

Leveraging Existing Community

Sometimes digital organizing isn't about building new community online but is all about leveraging your existing community by augmenting their experience. This can appear in a number of ways, like building out new tools or locating digital resources for the community. It can also be training your current community on online tools to make their work more efficient or impactful.

Locating or building out the right tools should take two main questions into account:
1) What do you need the community to impact?
2) What does the community need in order to make that impact?

To answer these questions you need to know what your goals and expectations are for the community. Then you need to listen. Don't just listen to every request, but also look for the underlying themes. Knowing your own goal should be fairly straightforward. Listening for what is truly needed requires a more nuanced approach.

The reality is, like all good organizing, you have to make some hard decisions. When asking people what they broadly want, you might get an overwhelming list of features that would be cost prohibitive to buy or build. You might also hear a lot of things that are "nice to haves" instead of "need to haves" to accomplish the goal. Nuanced listening is understanding if people understand the current resources. It might be more of a training issue than a features issue. Either way, you are the best one to interpret the data and make a decision that gets you closer to what you want.

Training on the Tools

During the 2012 campaign cycle I developed a wide range of trainings for digital staff, field staff, and volunteers. At the core of all of it, was empowering people to more effectively meet their goals and get President Obama another term in office. The trainings ranged from technical aspects of digital jobs, to social media for day-to-day organizing, to how to leverage campaign-built tools to augment traditional organizing.

The campaign's "Dashboard" organizing platform had many fits and starts. Or starts and fits. I had the privilege of working through a rolling series of trainings with the project managers, Jessica Morales Rocketto and Jeff Gabriel. It was a piece of technology meant to unify systems and make the overall experience for organizers better. For many of the early users, I thank you still. We learned training by training, and from launch successes and setbacks, how to make things better. However, some of those setbacks made a fair share of supporters hesitant to use the tools because at a small scale, their current hacks around the previously broken system were working. I knew a thing or two about that.

When I was a field organizer for Obama '08 no one had showed me the value of marking volunteers for their shifts in the database and when you had only three or four consistent volunteers, it didn't matter. As the campaign escalated, we needed to confirm and manage volunteers better. It easily clicked since we had data on who had done what in the past and that made it easier to prioritize whom to call back for what. It changed our world and ability to hit, and then exceed, goals.

I took that knowledge and worked with more senior organizing leadership. I laid down the value and got their buy in. From there we got the buy in of other levels of leadership, and the trainings met far less resistance. It was organizing the organizers to help the other organizers more effectively do their work. Yes, very meta and a great example of how approaching even digital training as an organizer, you see that empowerment has an exponential effect.

Digital Organizing with Partners

Digital tools have allowed us to amplify and spread messages like never before. In an instant, an issue hashtag can be trending, a video can gain thousands of views, and an image can become a meme. When done well, it is rarely a fluke. More often than not, there was a plan that crossed between good strategy and good digital organizing.

Sometimes when we are organizing community we are organizing a community of communities. It is not just leveraging one immediate network, but thinking about how can you work in a way the leverage multiple entities' online presence. When working this way, you should always keep in mind what would make the ask easiest for you if you were the one being asked for something.

Keep the ask clear and consistent. Are you asking for groups to join for one particular day or action, or a longer-term commitment? Be sure to ask yourself if you could build a better long-term relationship by asking for everything up front or by having one successful day that others would want to be part of in the future. There isn't one right answer but you should be thoughtful about what you need and want both in the short and long-term plan for your community.

Try to package things in as simple of a system as possible. Remember that every barrier you set between the content and whoever needs to grab and schedule it, the less likely it is to happen. If you have a really clear goal and the partners are needed to get there, then make that clear. We all respond better to knowing how we can be directly impactful.

Digital Organizing Thoughts and Principles

Model what works well in person when you can and decide where it makes sense. Does your organization or campaign have chapters? Then make sure your replicate and respect that structure online.

Are there founding principles and ideas to your organization that people connect to? If yes, make sure you replicate those principles in online community with your language and behavior.

Don't fear the small ask. Sometimes people are afraid to make a small ask for fear of losing a supporter. This ask could be to share content or change their profile image. If you've built meaningful relationship with someone, it is really about the right ask, at the right time, to the right audience. I've met a few major donors over the years that loved when we asked them to tweet. It allowed them to leverage their social clout (klout) and gave them another way to engage with a cause they loved when their schedule didn't allow for anything else.

Empower people where you can. Most people thrive with respect and responsibility. Let them and your organization thrive.

At the end of the day, good digital organizing is just good organizing online using online tools. The human element still applies and is what impacts change.

Digital organizing and the role of a digital organizer is all about intentionally building relationships and leveraging community power to work together in a coordinated way for a coordinated cause. You can use digital organizing to build a new online community. It is also about leveraging your existing community or augmenting their experience. You can and should approach coordinating groups with a human centric organizing model. Good digital organizing will help you execute your plans and meet your goals to make the impact the world needs you to make.

2016: A Vision of Hope

The 2016 electoral cycle was hard for anyone with social, progressive views. But somewhere wrapped up in that mess, I had the privilege of working with a new political start-up, Vote.org, as well as some very successful local issue races with the firm 50+1 strategies, led by Nicole Derse. It is hard to write about the positives in these times when overall, many issues I hope to leave a positive impact on are now headed into a defensive mode instead of moving forward with progress. But so much magic happened with Vote.org, it really was (and is) replicable magic.

Vote.org is led by a goals-focused visionary named Debra Cleaver, and along the way we were joined by Raven Brooks, formerly with Netroots Nation. At the center of it, one of the things that drew me to Vote.org was a focus on goals and only doing work that moved the goals. I joined the team about 10 weeks before Election Day with a daunting task: We were going to run two massive programs and had only a loose foundation.

I joined at the point that the organization had two-and-a-half full-time staff, including the Executive Director, Debra. Her excellence of focus meant Vote.org has been hugely successful in building simple online tools to drive voter registration and SEO to drive traffic through those tools. That success meant program one would be running a very rigorous GOTV program to try and turn out the 1.5 million and growing list of voters using SMS and email. Program two would be running what could be a groundbreaking new SMS voter registration drive. We had two very simple driving goals.

1. Register as many people to vote in every state by their deadline.
2. Get as many people out to vote as we can.

The SMS voter registration is where I draw so much hope. Because of Debra's vision and my experience scaling projects in a goal-based fashion, we were able to shift costs and reach voters who would likely have been missed. The plan was to use the peer-to-peer text messaging service called Hustle. You may have heard about because it is what Bernie's campaign built their SMS peer-to-peer campaign on. Lost in election lore is the reality that the Obama 2012 team used some of the same technology in the closing days of 2012 GOTV. We were going to use a large team of volunteers or staff to contact communities that are often missed by traditional field and mail tactics. Traditional voter registration has the following costs as verified by the Analyst Institute:

- Mail-based outreach: $18 on average per net new registration
- Site-based outreach: $25 on average per net new registration
- Online-outreach: $94 on average per net new registration
- Door-to-door canvassing: $715 on average per net new registration

Our goal was to get in lower than site-based costs for our total costs.

We had some huge fits and starts, but never lost focus of the key goals including knowing whether or not we were on track to hit the daily and weekly milestones to make the voter registration successful. Our first start was working with a talented young man who had worked in Bernie world but didn't have the experience needed to scale a new volunteer program with a wildly short window. The steps needed to get to scale weren't lining up so we brought onboard a professional organizing firm. Then a week into work, they were behind on tool and program knowledge, which left them behind on some key milestones they needed to hit. Our plan was to start by reaching a few thousand people a day, then leap to tens of thousands, and ultimately have days reaching several hundred thousand people. The milestones to success were clear.

When the professional firm was behind, we were left with a pretty big, now what? We knew if we had to open our own text message center, it would leave us behind on our milestones to run a successful GOTV. Debra and I were able to have honest triage conversations because we knew our goals #1 and #2. We decided that having more people to GOTV was more important than a lot of pre-planning on GOTV and we could start closer to election day if needed. So on a Sunday night, we were able to connect with the leader of the Citizen Engagement Lab, Jackie Mahendra, who knew the value of this program and could assist with space for us to give our third major shift to get on track to meeting milestones in as many weeks in scaling this project.

That Tuesday, we had 30 people logging into computers and learning the system. We made the goals clear to everyone; our ultimate goal was to register as many people as possible. Together, we would make sure the experience of people who received the text messages was as positive as it could be. We would use analytics on scripts to maximize the conversion of messages to registrations.

That week, this team of nonpolitical folks who had been mostly recruited from a local LGTBQ group, took ownership of the program. It was probably the most well gelled and functional GOTV teams I've been a part of. It was also the most diverse ethnically, and across the LGTBQ spectrum team that I've had the privilege of working on. Because we were clear with the goals and empowered others to own the goals, we were reaching milestones and quickly let the failing firm go.

Something beautiful happened. This team of non-campaign cycle folks took ownership and we didn't just get on track but far exceeded our goals. A team led by Daniella, Charlie, Kahlil, Kelly, Felix, and Kit shifted engagement for millions of Americans we connected with over the cycle. On the way, they hit these milestones for connecting with communities:

- 4,250,000 peer-to-peer text messages sent during GOTV and Voter Registration
- We registered over 26,000 new voters.
- $8.11 per voter registered far exceeding our goals and made the program more successful dollar for dollar than mail - the previous best.

It leaves me with a deep belief that running a project or campaign focused on your goals can accomplish major things. Good organizing and empowering people will ultimately lead to positive change in the world. I hope for you, this book helps you do more of that

NOTES

NOTES

ABOUT THE AUTHOR

Brad has been driving engagement via the internet for almost a decade. For the past eight years, he's been working on electoral issues in a variety of roles from in person organizing to helping shape President Obama's 2012 battleground state digital strategy. He was the founding Digital Strategist for Organizing for Action, and the Digital Manager for the Obama-Biden 2012 Inaugural National Day of Service. In 2010 he oversaw regional digital strategy for the Democratic National Committee working with Senatorial, Gubernatorial, and Congressional races. In 2014 he supported CredoSuperPAC driving the digital side of their field campaign. Recently, he directed the rebuilding of the digital department the Rainforest Action Network, an international advocacy organization. During the 2016 cycle, he took on local and national issues helping drive engagement for school board, propositions, and local elections. All of that in the background while running groundbreaking registration and GOTV programs as Head of Engagement for Vote.org.

43866200R00081

Made in the USA
San Bernardino, CA
30 December 2016